The
Simple Home

The Spirit of Simple Living™

The Simple Home

A Faith-Filled Guide to Simplicity, Peace, and Joy in Your Home

Sharon Hanby-Robie

GuidepostsBooks™

New York, New York

The Simple Home

ISBN 0-8249-4702-9

Published by GuidepostsBooks
16 East 34th Street, New York, New York 10016
www.guidepostsbooks.com

Distributed by Ideals Publications, a Guideposts company
535 Metroplex Drive, Suite 250, Nashville, Tennessee 37211

GuidepostsBooks, Ideals, and *The Spirit of Simple Living*
are registered trademarks of Guideposts, Carmel, New York.

ACKNOWLEDGMENTS

Every attempt has been made to credit the sources of copyrighted material used in this book. If any such acknowl-
edgment has been inadvertently omitted or miscredited, receipt of such information would be appreciated.

Scripture quotations marked (KJV) are taken from *The King James Version of the Bible.*

Scripture quotations marked (NAS) are taken from the *New American Standard Bible,* © The Lockman
Foundation, 1960, 1962, 1963, 1968, 1971, 1972, 1973, 1975, 1977. Used by permission.

Scripture quotations marked (NIV) are taken from *The Holy Bible, New International Version.* Copyright
© 1973, 1978, 1984 International Bible Society. Used by permission of Zondervan Bible Publishers.

Scripture quotations marked (NKJV) are taken from *The Holy Bible, New King James Version.* Copyright
© 1997, 1990, 1985, 1983 by Thomas Nelson, Inc.

Scripture quotations marked (RSV) are taken from the *Revised Standard Version of the Bible.* Copyright ©
1946, 1952, 1971 by Division of Christian Education of the National Council of Churches of Christ in the U.S.A.
Used by permission.

Library of Congress Cataloging-in-Publication Data

Hanby-Robie, Sharon.
The simple home : a faith-filled guide to simplicity, peace, and joy
in your home / Sharon Hanby-Robie.
    p. cm. — (The spirit of simple living)
Includes bibliographical references (p.   ) and index.
ISBN 0-8249-4702-9 (alk. paper)
1. Interior decoration—Psychological aspects. 2. Christian life. I. Title. II. Series.
NK2113.H258 2006
747.01'9—dc22
                                                    2006005588

Cover photograph © Stockbyte/SuperStock
Author photograph © Lynn Noble
Designed by Marisa Jackson

Printed and bound in Italy
1 3 5 7 9 10 8 6 4 2

To the publisher and editors at GuidepostsBooks,
I send an enormous thank you.

To my "dreamer" husband, Dave, without whom I would never attempt
to climb the mountain, thank you for your ever-inspiring faith in me.

I thank Patty, my assistant, for her daily encouragement and diligent
work; Cris Bolley, for her excellent edits and opinions;
and Deb Strubel, for her ability to define and develop ideas
in a way that makes the big picture crystal clear.

Giving thanks, honor, and praise to my Lord, for His gracious love that
inspires all creativity, wisdom, and understanding.

Contents

Introduction

For in him we live, and move, and have our being. . . .

—ACTS 17:28 (KJV)

God created us and He is close to us. He is sovereign and personal and He cares how we live. The Bible says in Acts 17:26 that God determined times *when* we would live and the exact places *where* we would live. Verse 27 (NIV) says, "God did this so that men would seek him and perhaps reach out for him and find him, though he is not far from each one of us."

Isn't it comforting and wonderful to know there is a Being greater than ourselves who is in control of the universe—and also in charge of the extent of our lives and the exact places where we live? Imagine how different life would be if we let the Creator of the universe not only rule our lives but our homes as well.

Our homes are the only environment over which we have control. As storms brew outside, our homes should be our personal sanctuaries. When you think about the word *sanctuary*, what do you feel? For most of us sanctuary is synonymous with simplicity. Creating the simple home is not only practical for everyday living but also vital to spiritual health. And it is available to everyone regardless of economic status, demanding schedules, and spiritual beliefs. Building awareness of our spiritual selves and integrating that awareness into the way we live is important—it connects us directly with our Creator and allows us to feel peace within ourselves.

As you read the steps for creating the simple home, you will have the opportunity to determine what is valuable to you and to make changes that exemplify the important things in life. For example, as you examine how you are living now, you may realize that you have unintentionally made it more difficult to maintain optimum spiritual health and peacefulness with a cluttered home.

If you are like me, you are probably awed by how God is able to manage the universe while we can hardly manage our homes. Personally, I think it would be interesting to see what the insides of my closets and cupboards would look like if I asked God to help me weed out and organize them.

At the heart of it, we all yearn for a simpler life. We want a life that is free from busyness and distraction and is filled with the people, activities, and things we love. We hope for a life that actually allows time for the abundant and true way of living that most of us can only imagine.

In that imagined life, my "to-do" list no longer resembles an unending string of seemingly impossible-to-accomplish tasks, such as:

Someday, I'm going to clean out the garage.
Someday, I'm going to organize my closet.
Someday, I'm going to paint the guest room.
Someday, I'm going to replace that old chair.
Someday, I will catch up on sorting and filing old tax papers.
Someday, I will invite dear friends I haven't seen in years to tea.
Someday . . . when I find the time. . . .

Have you, like me, ever wondered what the point is of having a home if we never have time to really enjoy it, let alone care for it? My hope is that this book will help you cut down your "to-do" list to a manageable size and make your home closer to your ideal. For me, Charles Keeler, poet, playwright and chief advocate of the Arts and Crafts movement in California, says it best:

> The ideal home is one in which the family may be most completely sheltered to develop in love, graciousness, and individuality, and which is at the same time most accessible to friends, toward whom hospitality is as unconscious and spontaneous as it is abundant. Emerson says that the ornament of a house is the friends who frequent it.
>
> —Charles Keeler, *The Simple Home*

Can you believe that the above description was written in 1906? It's almost funny. Here I am wishing for the simpler days of long ago only to find that they, too, were pining for simplicity.

If it's not the era that makes things so complicated, then what is it? If the home is the only environment that we have any control over, we must start making changes to improve that environment. Ultimately, we each must take personal responsibility and begin to make positive changes so that we can have the deeper desires of our hearts.

As an interior designer, what I hear from most people is that they just want a home that is pretty enough for them to feel comfortable entertaining, and easy enough to care for so that they don't feel like a slave to it. They want a place where family is nourished and friends feel welcome. Or as Charles Keeler also wrote, "In such a home, inspiring in its touch with art and books, glorified by mother love and child sunshine, may the human spirit grow in strength and grace to the fullness of years."

God made us—God is perfect, therefore, we all desire perfection. The problem is that this is earth and not heaven. Although we may not be able to have heaven on earth, we can have order. And that may be close enough to perfection to work. However, order looks as different to each of us as our personalities are different. My personality does not allow me to function well or creatively in chaos. Before I can begin doing anything productive, I need a clutter-free environment.

Unfortunately, this usually means that the rest of the house gets overlooked during the process. *But that's okay.* At one time, I could not say that. It would have been difficult for me to allow areas of my house to lose order while I was working creatively in another part. But I have learned that I cannot do it all and that I must make choices that make sense for me today.

As you begin this journey to create a simpler home, remember to be easy on yourself: Rome wasn't built in a day and neither was chaos tamed. Bringing simplicity and order to your home is a process that develops over time. The key to success will be to clarify your "big-picture" plan and implement it in small manageable portions. By doing this, you will find it is possible, in your own way, to create a sanctuary that meets the needs of all who reside there.

—*Sharon Hanby-Robie*

The
Simple Home

PART ONE

The Purpose of a Simple Home

THE FIRST STEP in bringing simplicity into your home is to define what it is you hope will take place within its walls. Many people try to fit their lives into the premolded floor plan of their homes without even thinking through whether it makes sense for the way they want to live. In this first step, I will show you ways to think outside of the blueprint and also to search inside your heart to identify the best uses of the home you have been given to enjoy.

Every Home Has a Mission

A mission statement acts as both a harness
and a sword—harnessing you to what is true about
your life and cutting away all that is false.

—LAURIE BETH JONES, *THE PATH: CREATING YOUR MISSION STATEMENT
FOR WORK AND FOR LIFE*

Just for a moment, pretend your home is a business. Most businesses have a mission statement, which is an overarching statement of purpose. If you were writing the mission statement for your home, what would it be? Think about it. Would your mission be to provide an environment of peace, comfort, safety, and joy? Defining and knowing the purpose for your home is vital to *creating* a simple home.

I live in Lancaster, Pennsylvania, which has a large Amish population. I have always admired the Amish. They are a self-sufficient society, whose homes are truly simple. They understand the value of simplicity. They believe in giving to God, their community, and taking care of each other. As in Christ's time, their church is actually their home. Each Sunday a different family opens its home for church. If you were Amish, one of the defining purposes of your home would be to accommodate the community for church. That would certainly have an effect on the choices you make for designing and furnishing your home, wouldn't it?

The simple yet abundant life of the Amish can be attractive. Their community is known to grow from the outside by three percent a year. Newcomers are drawn to this lifestyle because they are searching for a simpler, more relevant way to live.

An interesting statistic about the Amish—they have the highest success rate when it comes to starting new businesses. They have figured out how to meet modern-day needs regardless of their two-hundred-year-old style of living. But their way of life is not mine. God gave me the gift of creating beautiful interiors. I would not be happy in the starkness of an Amish home.

Too often, we define our home by someone else's rules or purpose. We compare our home with those of our friends, parents, community, or the latest trendy style, rather than evaluate how it meets our needs. Sometimes our expectations for our homes are impractical for real, everyday life. Perusing any number of home magazines will yield plenty of ideas, but few are likely to help us simplify our homes.

> Too often we define our home by someone else's rules or purpose, rather than evaluating how it meets our needs.

SIMPLICITY IS ALWAYS SATISFYING

As an interior designer, I am expected to have a beautiful, picture-perfect home like those shown in expensive home magazines. The reality is that when I return home after a long day I am not in the mood to do overtime. What I want is simply a comfortable place to relax! And I have accomplished that for the most part. My home is a calm place.

As a hyperactive, 24/7 kind of gal, I need that calming space. My heart would love to live at the beach, but living in an inland city, it must content itself with treasures from the beach. My home is best described as having colors of the sea and sky, adorned with the simple beauty that God created in seashells. Finishing touches include a few paintings from local artists, pretty pillows, and photos. My style is uncluttered—with one exception. Our two cats are allowed to have their toys and scratch pads scattered about as they choose.

My home is my sanctuary. I spend so much time with people every day that my home is my retreat, which is made complete with dear friends and family. And most of them comment about how peaceful it is. Purpose accomplished! So it's okay if it's not perfectly organized and there is still a closet, basement, and garage to be cleaned or laundry to be done.

For my own home, my mission statement is as follows:

I want my home to be ordered in such a way that it reflects the beauty and depth of our Lord's creation. I want it to be functional, provide safety and comfort, and yet remain gracious enough to soothe the senses and inspire dreams.

Living in a simple home offers us the freedom to focus on and enjoy one event, one day at a time. For me, to live a simple life is to handle what I can each day, and then plan for the big stuff. Soon I will have new carpeting installed. It will force me to clear items in my closets and empty the bookcase so it can be moved for the carpet installer. And someday, when I can wrangle my husband into helping, we'll attack the garage.

There was a time when I thought my house had to be perfectly clean all the time—perfectly decorated no matter if I could afford it. Thankfully, I got over that phase. The reality is that life has many phases and stages, and we will have a simpler and happier life if we accept graciously the particular phase or stage of life that we are in, and design our homes accordingly. And ultimately, isn't that the goal—a home that is comfortable, hospitable, and filled with people, food, laughter, and a godly spirit of love?

BEGIN WITH A MASTER PLAN

If you could have the perfect home, what would it look like? What would it feel like? How do you think it would change your life? If relationships are at the center of your heart, then making a place that is conducive to family and friends is one way to define the purpose of your home.

If working from home defines a major purpose of your house, as it did for an artist friend of mine, you may choose to use traditional areas in your house for new purposes. With her children grown and gone, my friend had the freedom of building her art studio in what had previously been the dining room and sunroom of her home. Her home also accommodated a grown son who had multiple sclerosis. As a result of her innovative use of space, her home became an art-filled and fun place to be.

Sometimes people lose perspective on the purpose of their home, and take perfection too far. I had a client many years ago who actually hung a rope across the entry to her newly decorated living room to keep her family out of it. How sad for her—and how sad for her children. Instead of being able to enjoy the fruits of her work, her family was forced to just observe them.

It is unfortunate when people think that designing and creating a beautiful way of living is all about possessions rather than the spirit of the home. No matter how beautiful a home may look, it is the warmth and the approachable attitude of those living inside that matter.

How does your home feel? What is your attitude when friends or strangers arrive unexpectedly? Are they always welcome? Or do you find yourself angry because they didn't call first? If so, why? Are you frustrated because they interrupted your schedule or because you wish you had time to straighten up the house?

And does your mission statement blend with the objectives of others who live in your home? Sometimes conflicting goals can cause the most strife. I'm a planner, so I'm reasonably well-organized. But I drive my husband Dave crazy because I am always early—he is always late. I hate clutter. He thrives on clutter. I was making myself nuts with his clutter. Notice I said that *I* was making myself nuts. Dave is who he is. I can't change that. But I can change my attitude.

> Creating a place that is conducive to family and friends is one way to define the purpose of your home.

We established a compromise. Dave's clutter stays upstairs and in the garage. When we know we need the guest room, he has to clean up. That's the deal. That way, I don't have to subject myself to his clutter. I just avoid going upstairs and we have a peaceful, clutter-free first floor.

My old attitude would have said, "I really don't care whether I can see it or not, I know it's there!" This new attitude is a choice, and a right spirit.

Charles Keeler understood clearly the purpose of home when he wrote, "Homemaking is one of the sacred tasks of life, for the home is the family temple, consecrated to the service of parents and offspring. As the strength of the state is founded upon family life, so is the strength of society based upon the home. The building of the home should be an event of profound importance." Although this quote was written a century ago, the truth of the sacred task of homemaking is still relevant and important to meeting the desires of our hearts. Make your home a sanctuary—a consecrated place, a place of refuge and protection.

As an interior designer, I can begin working on a home only after I define the purpose of the individual spaces. I start by asking some fundamental questions that you too can use as a starting point:

What is the style of the home?

What is the lifestyle of the family living here?

How are they functioning?

What functions must be performed in each room?

How can I better designate the existing spaces to meet the needs of the individuals?

SIMPLICITY MADE SIMPLE

PLAN a family powwow—even if it's just you and your spouse—or have a powwow with yourself! Have everyone prepare a list of the things that are most important to them regarding how the home should function.

RECOGNIZE that each family member has a perspective relative to his or her age group.

Although you cannot meet every need, **TAKE STEPS** to meet at least one need for each member of the family. For example, if you have children, provide a consistent place for doing homework.

START with an overall goal, then begin to narrow the purpose room by room.

ACKNOWLEDGE that God has a plan for all of us and that includes a plan for our home.

Dear Lord, thank You for giving me my home.

Please show me how to use my space

to meet my creative needs, and teach me

simple ways to demonstrate my love

for those with whom I share my home.

Room by Room

Unless the Lord builds the house,
those who build it labor in vain. . . .

—PSALM 127:1 (RSV)

Recently, I read an article about an architect who worked from home. He was handling the chaos of "stuff," such as his two daughters' schoolwork and art that was scattered all over the house. He was even reasonably okay with the fact that to start dinner he, his wife, and his daughters had to first clear the tabletop and countertops of clutter. But when all this stuff—including his wife's projects—started creeping into his home office, he lost it. He knew he had no choice but to draw the line.

Drawing the line meant creating more space for stuff. He decided to turn their ten-foot-by-thirteen-foot formal dining room into a family art studio and computer center. As I work with different people, it is apparent that the formal dining room is soon going to be extinct in most homes. It just doesn't make sense for today's simpler, less formal way of living. Since space has become such a commodity, turning your dining room into a room of usable, functioning convenience is nearly a requirement for sanity.

Converting a room into a family workspace does not need to cost a fortune. In fact, the architect I read about completed his project for $765. He made tabletops from thirty-two-inch-wide hollow birch interior doors. For organizing supplies, each workstation included four storage caddies that fit under the tables. He removed the wall-to-wall carpeting and replaced it with MDF (medium density fiberboard) sheets, which he finished with two coats of polyacrylic sealer to create a smooth, washable floor.

One of the amazing discoveries made as the family moved all the art supplies into the new room was that his wife had no idea she owned fifty paint brushes until she got them all into one space. I think most of us have no idea what we really own until we are forced to organize it. Too often, rather than look for a small specific item, it seems easier to buy another one.

EVALUATE THE USE OF YOUR SPACE

How does your home function? Is the kitchen table usually covered with homework and craft projects? Are your kitchen counters cluttered with piles of bills waiting to be paid and old newspaper articles and catalogs? What does your dining room look like? Would you be able to serve dinner there in a moment's notice, or would the exercise equipment need to be removed first?

If you are like most families, there is stuff everywhere. But when clutter is so out of control that the daily function of serving dinner requires the multistep process of clearing the table to set plates on it, it is time to make some changes. Changes may include rethinking the use of the rooms so that they actually make sense for how your family lives.

As mentioned, formal living rooms are a dead space that can become valuable if rethought. I recently completed a home makeover for some people. The couple was at the age where they thought life would be simpler. They had just retired. Their small

1970s two-story home had not been remodeled. It was their intention to finally redo the house to suit themselves. But like many best-laid plans, this one went awry. Both of their grown sons moved back home. One son came with his nine-year-old daughter.

I met Kate and Ken at this stage of the process. Their neighbor had recommended they call me. They were completely overwhelmed about working with an interior designer for the first time. "What does a designer do? Is this going to be expensive?" were just two of the questions they had. As we sat down in my studio for our first meeting, they attempted to give me a clear picture of how bad things really were. They kept repeating, "There is stuff and people everywhere! Everywhere—people and stuff! And how can you help?" I laughed, but they were not exaggerating.

Prior to the return of their sons, Kate had begun to create a peaceful sanctuary for herself in their previously formal living room. She purposely placed her piano where the natural light would reach the keyboard. She painted the walls one of her favorite colors—fuchsia—which, of course, her sons thought was awful, especially now that they had moved their computers into her space.

> Imagine how you would like to live in your home, and then make changes to create such a setting.

CLEAR AWAY THE CLUTTER

My first suggestion was to make several trips to the local dump or charity bin. The garage was full; the family room was an obstacle course of boxes, extra furniture, and too many long legs in one space as people tried to watch television. There wasn't a chair that Ken could call his own, which was a big issue for him since he was about to have hip replacement surgery. After six trips to the dump, they began to make a dent in the boxes.

My next suggestion for this old home was to replace all the flooring on the first floor with a beautiful wood-grained, natural-color laminate flooring, which could easily be installed and maintained. Out came the old, dreary wall-to-wall shag carpeting and the vinyl-tiled kitchen and foyer floors.

Since the kitchen and family room were nearly one room, we tackled the unsightly orange kitchen countertops, and replaced them with a warm, light-colored, multihued neutral. At the same time, we reconfigured the old, round dining counter extension with a cropped corner rectangle, creating more room for an additional chair in the family room. New paint and Luminette sheer verticals on the sliding doors made the family room a light-filled space that seemed larger and more cheerful.

Next came the new furniture. Knowing that it had to be durable and comfortable made choosing a large creamy leather sofa, chair and two ottomans the perfect solution for everyone. Leather easily wipes clean, yet is soft and inviting. The light-colored walls, furniture, and floor made the space feel more open, larger, and relaxing. A colorful area rug with matching runner and a brightly colored abstract painting completed the look of the family room.

As we were hanging the family pictures on the newly painted wall, Kate and Ken brought tears to my eyes as they told me how happy they were. They said I had heard their hearts' cry, helping them make sense of the chaos and accommodating everyone while still making it pretty. They said I helped them recognize their own needs, which was why they were able to make such a transformation.

Getting someone else's perspective often makes the process of simplifying and redoing a home much smoother. As an outsider, it was easy for me to make clear-cut suggestions on the elimination of unnecessary clutter because I was not emotionally attached to it. Yet even without an outsider's help, there's so much you can accomplish just by putting your mind to the task and letting your imagination run wild.

Cecile Andrews, author of *The Circle of Simplicity* and affiliated scholar at Seattle University, is developing a simplicity studies program. He says, "Simplicity is the examined life richly lived. It is asking ourselves what's important, what matters. We all think that someday we'll start living. But few of us feel fully alive."

Kate and Ken thought their time to personalize their home had finally come when the kids moved out; instead what they discovered is that living life to the fullest is learning to live the life God has given you. This time, this place, this family—no matter how it is defined—is the life God has chosen for you to live right now. Accepting it can be an enormous relief and blessing.

SIMPLICITY MADE SIMPLE

START by assessing your needs. Do you need an extra bedroom, a home entertainment area, an exercise space or an office? Take an inventory of all the tasks your family enjoys, such as crafting, sewing, music, and so forth.

ASK YOURSELF what the desired tasks will require. Do you need insulation to deaden the sound of drum practice or electronic games? Will you need appliances such as a refrigerator for serving drinks or food?

CONSIDER CONVERTING any room that is not used full-time into a space that will be used to the max.

BUILT-INS are a great way to better utilize the space you have. Built-in countertops and storage drawers provide plenty of room for organized creativity.

CONSIDER FUTURE FUNCTION. If your children are toddlers, it won't be long before they outgrow this phase and require homework space. Today's playroom may later be the teenager's hangout.

Did you know that **TOO MUCH STUFF** in your home can significantly increase the amount of housework you do? That alone should be enough incentive to get you started on the elimination process!

ENCOURAGE your children to have a "kids garage sale," and let them donate the funds to charity. This will help them to develop a spirit for giving and the discipline to live junk-free.

THE KEY to a room's functioning well is organization. Think about the tasks you want to accomplish in the room. Do you have everything you need? Sometimes it's the smaller, less significant tasks that take the most time because we waste so much time looking for what we need. If you have an hour of time to craft but waste it looking for your supplies, you no longer have an hour for fun.

Lord, give me wisdom to clear away those
things that distract me from what is important
to my life. Help me to rid myself of confusion
so that I can enjoy the creative use of my home.

The Heart of the Home

Ponder well on this point: the pleasant
hours of our life are all connected
by a more or less tangible link,
with some memory of the table.

—CHARLES PIERRE MONSELET (1825–1888)

When I read the above quotation, I was immediately transported to my childhood memories of sitting around the kitchen or dining room table. This was where life was lived. Meals at the kitchen table were boisterous and filled with laughter—occasionally to the dismay of my father. It wasn't often, but every once in a while Dad felt the need for a quiet dinner—a difficult challenge for our family of six children.

One evening in particular, Dad said, "The next person to laugh is going to bed without dinner!" At that moment, Mom lost it and burst out laughing as hard as she could. Of course, we all joined in laughing until we cried. Dad crumbled. And try as he might, he could not hold back the laughter as tears rolled down his face. It makes me sad to think how many families are missing out on the memory of being together each evening for a meal.

Our dining room table was a multipurpose space. During the many family celebrations and get-togethers, this was where we converged. Since our immediate family was so large, our home was where our extended family came to celebrate. Having several generations together at the table was an event in itself. I loved the discussions, both loud and soft, as we shared, learned, and simply lived together as family.

The dining room table was also the place where I cut my patterns for sewing and where freshly ironed clothes were placed for us to take to our rooms. It is where many homework projects were developed and refined. And most importantly to us children, where the weekend-long board games such as Monopoly were played. Our games included many neighbors, adults and children alike, as we played in teams for two to three days at a time without stopping! This tradition continues today on my mom's dining room table. It's exciting to watch as two new generations join in the fun.

GIVE YOURSELF SOME SPACE

The kitchen has and always will be the center or heart of the home. In most families, the kitchen is used more than any other space in the home. Simplicity can turn the daily task of cooking into an eagerly anticipated event. Thoughtful organization of workspaces will facilitate helping hands if people do not have to cross over each other to get the items they need.

For example, a baking center can be defined in any existing kitchen. Putting all the baking supplies, mixers, and measuring cups in one location will simplify the steps it takes to make biscuits or mix a dessert. Another area can be defined for chopping vegetables by placing a cutting board and colander near the drawer that holds knives and utensils for cooking. Look for ways to allow two or more people to work in the kitchen without needing to step into each other's space. This can be accomplished in even the smallest kitchens.

Sometimes it is possible to expand the kitchen into an adjacent room. I love the fact that today we are rediscovering the hearth room of Colonial times. Many new homes now include a fireplace and sitting area in the kitchen. Others no longer have a wall between the kitchen and family room—creating an open space that is perfect for today's way of living. Many people ask me to help rework their old kitchen and family rooms into hearth rooms. One such person walked into my studio one day, late in August, and asked if I could come to her home *now*.

Patty actually meant for me to drop everything I was doing and come home with her. She wasn't being rude—she was just excited. She wanted to begin renovations right then so she could have them done and ready for the Christmas holidays. Well, I couldn't really go just then, but we did schedule an appointment for soon afterward.

The kitchen has and always will be the center or heart of the home.

Patty and her husband Brad live in a wonderful old neighborhood with their three daughters and a dog. Brad insisted on being at all our meetings because he had not been involved the previous time they had work done in the house. As a result, he had no input and there were things that were important to him that did not get addressed.

At our initial meeting, we determined that to accommodate their lifestyle, it made sense to turn the family room into an extension of the kitchen. We moved the kitchen table into the adjacent family room. As a result, we found room in the kitchen for the much-needed island, which provided additional counter space and storage. We placed the kitchen table near the sliding doors so they were able to enjoy the view of the backyard while eating dinner.

Patty had always loved French country styling, which often uses contrasting light and dark shades in the room, such as dark beams against pale plaster ceilings and intensely happy-colored provincial printed rugs against dark wooden floors. Flowers are an integral part of the French country area rugs. Themes that are often used in this fine carpeting include vines, flowers, and leaves that are sometimes arranged in geometric patterns, borders, or striped sections. Colors comprise a range of earthy and bright tones: balmy golds, grass greens, brilliant azure blues, deep rustic reds, sunny yellows, browns, and beige. It was the perfect choice for Patty's new kitchen space because it is inviting, friendly, and cheerful. Someone once said that if you change your outer environment, your inner environment will follow. Creating an attractive, pretty space in the room where Patty's family spent so much time would help them enjoy being there.

> If you change your outer environment, your inner environment will follow.

In order to create more space for the kitchen and eating area, it was necessary to remove a swivel chair and an overstuffed leather sofa. The sofa was moved to the formal living room, which was to become the new family room. We agreed that in place of the sofa we'd put two smaller chairs and ottomans, which still provided a cozy sitting area near the fireplace.

The room had a hardwood floor, so I knew a rug would set the stage for the new space. I arranged for a meeting to show them the options I had found. Brad was having a hectic day and was running late, so by the time he arrived, Patty, their three daughters, and I had already found a beautiful French country-style hooked rug with a colorful floral pattern and black background. The yellow, red, green, and deep orchid shades were perfect for their decorating scheme. And the black combined with the multitones would be wonderful at hiding soil. That translates into less cleaning and shampooing of the carpet—a good choice for a busy mom and family. When Brad arrived, it was easy to see that he too thought it was a good choice.

Using the foundation of the colors of the rug to work from, it was easy to choose fabrics and paint colors for the room. The chairs we purchased were a pair of upholstered-to-the-floor French country wing chairs with dressmaker skirts. We had them covered in a beautiful woven botanical print in yellow and white. Of course, we also had them stain-proofed. To the chairs we added two red leather tufted ottomans that easily would take the abuse of shoed feet. They are also great for holding a serving tray for entertaining or snacks.

We completed the seating area in the new kitchen space with two country-style wood chairs with fun cushions to complement the décor. A new print of a French floral market and two new lamps were the perfect jewels for making this room sparkle. The expanded kitchen with its cozy seating area now allows for extending the kitchen table. The new arrangement has given this family the room it needed for living every day the way they want.

SIMPLICITY MADE SIMPLE

Think of your life first in the **TRAFFIC PATTERNS** of daily living. Only then can you decide how everyday demands can be accommodated in your plan.

CONSIDER CREATING WIDE-OPEN SPACES by eliminating unnecessary walls. This makes it easier for the family to get together and entertain.

ESTABLISH DIFFERENT ZONES in your existing spaces—especially in large open rooms. We accomplished this for Patty and Brad by placing an area rug under the two chairs and ottomans. That helped to anchor the conversation area while providing a beautiful but sound-absorbing insulator for this busy room.

TEST your new floor-plan ideas either on paper in a scaled drawing, or place paper cutouts and boxes on the floor to see how you like the new plan.

Don't forget to **USE THE VERTICAL SPACE** in your room. By adding shelving, hooks, bulletin and chalkboards, along with hanging storage and organizers, you will gain hundreds of additional square feet for all your family's things.

ALLOW YOURSELF TO DREAM a little about how you would like to live. For example, if you would like your family to spend more time playing board games or putting puzzles together, then be sure to provide an easily accessible place to do so. Patty and Brad added built-in bookcases with cabinets below to house games and puzzles. The bookshelves hold their most often used resources and are perfect for displaying family photos.

Consider setting aside an area or **ROOM JUST FOR PRAYER**, to make it easier to keep prayer as an important part of your family life. It can be a place where the family members can come alone or together before God for praying, praising, singing, or simply to quiet themselves before the Lord.

> Father, we acknowledge that You are the
> center of our home, and through You comes
> our daily bread for both physical and
> spiritual growth. We ask that You bless both
> the food and the fellowship that are at our table.

Friends Are Welcome Here

Offer hospitality to one another without grumbling.
Each one should use whatever gift
he has received to serve others,
faithfully administering God's grace
in its various forms.

—1 PETER 4:9–10 (NIV)

As a child growing up in the inner city of Cleveland, Ohio, I didn't have much, which wasn't a problem when I was young. However, as a teenager I began to feel embarrassed by our humble abode. I was fortunate to attend an all-girls' school in the suburbs. The problem arose when I started to date. Since most of the guys I was meeting came from the suburbs, I was nervous just thinking about them coming to my neighborhood to pick me up for a date. My home couldn't compete with the community where they lived.

I had one friend who understood. She lived a few blocks from me and attended the same high school. In fact, there was one guy in particular whom she wanted to date. Unfortunately, he did not have a car, which meant the only way she could go out with him was if I agreed to go with his friend who did have a car. She was excited, and I was apprehensive thinking about our double date.

As we pondered our dilemma, we remembered that a year or two before, the all-boys' high school had done an amazing job of transforming their school into a castle. They accomplished this by building an elaborate façade to completely hide the front of the building. Sandy and I considered building similar façades for our own homes. As we giggled and dreamed, we came to the realization that it would be necessary to hide the entire neighborhood! Obviously, that would be out of the question.

In retrospect, just building a façade for our individual homes was also out of the question. We had no choice but to accept the fact that this was where we lived and this was who we were, and we were okay. That was a better choice and a good lesson for life.

To some degree, our homes are a reflection of who we are. Others perceive how we care for our homes and even the colors we choose to paint them as reflecting our personality. Not that I am suggesting we play the game of "keeping up with the Joneses." Rather, we are to be good stewards of what God has blessed us with and make the most of those blessings. Even the most modest home can be well-kept and inviting to its visitors.

I suggest that you take a walk around your neighborhood and notice which homes are most attractive to you. Be honest, you know that some homes have always caught your lingering gaze. This time, stop and take a moment to evaluate what specifically draws your attention to a particular home.

Is it color? Usually that's the first thing we notice about a house, but go a bit further. Is it the walkway? Does it beckon you to the door either by design or by the beautiful planters placed along the path? Is there an inviting bench that is calling

> Even the most modest home can be well-kept and inviting to its visitors.

you to come rest? Perhaps it's simply the way the home is cared for—the walk is swept clean, the shrubbery is trimmed, and the flowers on the door's wreath are your favorite kind.

On your walk, look for your favorite house in the neighborhood. In other words, if you could choose to live in any home, to which house would you direct your friends and neighbors, pretending it was yours? Now for the big question: Did you send them to your home? If not, then keep reading.

ENTRYWAY EXPRESSIONS

The entryways to our homes can make a statement about the quality of life we enjoy inside its walls, but many of us seldom use our front door. Instead we enter the house through the garage or back door, which means we hardly have an idea of the actual condition of our front entrance.

I once considered taking a machete with me to the home of a particular client. One could hardly pass through the overgrown shrubbery, let alone walk along the brick pathway that had long ago lost its footing. Yet the inside of the home was attractive and well-kept. But if you didn't know that, you would have thought otherwise by the appearance of the front yard. The reality is that these were not outdoorsy people. They did not have a garden. They were not interested in doing yard work. They hired a neighbor to mow their lawn. And they never used their front door. It never occurred to them that there was anything that needed attending. When it came time to sell their home, I encouraged them to hire someone to chop down the jungle. They laughed—but they took my advice.

Speaking of selling a home, this is a good state of mind to put yourself into when thinking about the entryways of your home. Pretend that you are about to list your home for sale. I'm the real estate agent that you have hired to work with you. As your agent, I may make the following suggestions: repaint your front door and, if needed, replace the weather stripping on it. While we are at it, replace the hardware—handle and key lock, and add a brass kickplate. Find some pretty potted plants and a nice doormat—perhaps one of those new metal doormats with a welcome sign in the center.

Or think about all the model homes you have visited. They quickly got your attention because they were pushing your emotional home buttons long before you walked through the door. How were they able to do this? *The point is that it doesn't take a lot to make a big difference.*

Most of my friends enter through the back door of my house. Until I built a screened-in porch, they came through our garage! That was not a pretty sight. The garage is my husband's domain, and as I mentioned before, he is a pack rat. Finding your way through the maze of his stuff is daring in itself, which is fine if you are looking for an adventure.

I wish my husband would let me take him to the home of another client of mine who realized that his garage was also the entrance most used by everyone. Ed cleared a path from the outside door to the inside and then decorated it as if it were an entry hall. He placed an inexpensive Oriental-style runner on the floor. Then he added a small console table with a lamp and even hung a nice print above it. As you enter, you are pleasantly surprised at this simple but worthwhile effort he has made to make you feel welcome. In the evenings, the light of the lamp greets you with a cozy glow. It's amazing how simple it was for Ed to make such an impression on his visitors.

Viewed from the outside, a home can reveal how well it functions not only as basic shelter but also as a gracious and vibrant part of our lives.

> Decorative objects and collections give a house charm and a distinctive character.

SIMPLICITY MADE SIMPLE

YOUR EXTERIOR DOOR should provide draft-free protection. To ensure that it does, replace weather stripping with foam or beaded metal strips. While you're at it, be sure your rubber sweep on the bottom of the door is still intact and working effectively. If not, dirt caught under your door may cause a draft, which can be costly with today's energy prices.

YOU HAVE MANY CHOICES other than wood for a handsome front door that is easy to care for, such as steel or fiberglass. Most are insulated with a foam core to better protect against inclement weather. Steel is great—it just requires painting periodically. Fiberglass doors are lightweight and virtually maintenance free. They are easily stained with a wood color and they don't swell the way wooden doors do.

If possible, **ADD AN OVERHANG** above your front door. It not only will protect your door but also will provide a nice covering for guests during rough weather.

For a beautiful walkway, **CONSIDER PAVING STONES**. They install quickly, are durable, and are moderately priced. My patio and back walkway are made of pavers. The only maintenance they require is an occasional addition of sand for leveling beneath the spot where they settle. Other than that, a little spray of herbicide every now and then keeps them weed free. But be sure to read the instructions on your herbicide as it can be harmful to pets.

DON'T FORGET ABOUT OUTDOOR LIGHTING. Today it is easy to light your path with solar-powered lighting. It is easy to install and available in a variety of prices and styles. It's a simple way to make a big impact on your home's entry.

Repairs to existing structures do not require any **NEW CODE COMPLIANCE**. However, before beginning any new building or expansion of a walkway, be sure to check with your local code department. Most have very strict codes regarding any changes to existing structures or building new projects.

TRY ADDING a bench, baskets of flowers, or a new welcome mat for a refreshing change of pace. My assistant Patty used an old chair and placed a pretty potted plant on the seat. She even added a small decorative table alongside it. Another friend of mine decorates his front porch every year with gauzy curtains tied back at the poles and then sets out a little bistro table and chairs. Every time I pass his home, it makes me smile.

> Lord, help me to welcome guests into my home.
> Let others see that Your goodness abides
> in this place, and let Your light draw them
> into my peaceful home.

Mission: Art

Creating a beautiful home is a high achievement;

enjoying it is the art of living.

—ALEXANDRA STODDARD, *CREATING A BEAUTIFUL HOME*

Esther and Ed have been clients of mine for more than twenty years. I have watched their two sons grow from adorable little boys to strong, amazing men. I am honored to have been a part of their lives for all these years.

Last year, I helped Esther and Ed with what they think will be the last home they will build. It was the second house I worked on with them, although we actually decorated their first home twice, after a freak fire destroyed two-thirds of it.

As I walked through the ashes with them after the fire, I remember Ed rejoicing over the discovery of a candlestick that had belonged to Esther's mother. The heat of fire had reshaped it. Today it adorns their dining table as a shining symbol of all that is good in life. Though bent and burnished, the candlestick is a reminder that no one was injured in the fire. They are thankful that when their son opened the garage that fateful day he was not hurt as the flames burst out, and no one else was home.

Working with Ed and Esther is a delight. They are a wonderful family and good people. When their children were young we designed spaces that met the needs of growing young boys without neglecting the passions of the parents. When they rebuilt, they added a new master wing and a music niche for Esther.

I was excited at the prospect of working on their new home. This home would be different from the previous home. This time there would be no children living at home, and Ed and Esther could now make room for their love of art.

They collect art and are blessed with the professional advice of Esther's brother, who is a curator at a major art museum. Of course there had to be some financial compromises. After all, the kids came first. But they managed to collect a few nice pieces. When their children went off to college, the collecting of art became much more subdued—a natural result of college tuition bills. With their youngest in law school and their oldest doing well with a fine career ahead of him, it was *finally* time for Esther and Ed. They could now focus on their own passions, which meant they could enjoy the pleasure of expanding their art collection.

PLAN FOR THE LIFE YOU WANT TO ENJOY

Simplifying your life gives you the ability to enjoy what you truly love. You simplify life by making choices that make sense for the way you want to live. If the beauty of art is an important element for you, then plan for it, both financially and physically. You don't have to spend large sums of money to indulge your passion. Find beauty in imperfection; many objects show their beauty in their history.

I love art too, but not so much that I turn it into an investment hobby. Instead, I have taken advantage of many local artists' work. That way I can have original artwork without spending a fortune. It also makes the local artists very happy—unfortunately, the adage of "starving artist" is still a reality.

As we began to plan Ed and Esther's new home, we knew that one purpose of this home would be to show art beautifully and simply. They both thought they were ready for more color in their decorating scheme; they were considering the use of color on the walls, which reflected the current design trend in home fashion. However, too much color on the walls would compete for attention with the art. We reached a compromise that everyone loved: we painted the foyer a medium shade of gold, the dining room a paler shade of green, and the main room the same as the foyer. These colors provided a backdrop for art while still filling in the blanks with just enough color to make the room feel complete.

Wall space was another significant decision. Although Esther and Ed wanted an open floor plan, they also needed lots of large wall space to hang what they hoped would be a growing collection. That's a tough objective, but with cooperation and determination, we found a way to accomplish the task. I started by drawing to scale each individual room and area within the home. Using most of the existing furniture and only adding what was absolutely necessary to finish spaces, we were able to put together a workable plan.

> Having a plan simplifies the overall process of creating a home you love.

Then I placed the existing artwork into the spaces, taking into consideration future acquisitions of art. Having a plan simplified the overall process. By defining the overarching purpose and detailing the individual spaces, we could easily build a home that would meet their needs.

LIGHT UP YOUR LIFE

Among the other things we needed to consider for the existing and future art was lighting. Without light we cannot see the wonders that are before us. This is as true in our spiritual growth as it is in our physical world. We need light to clearly see the truth of what is beautiful in our lives.

Lighting art is an art in itself—and a tricky and often costly one as well. Plan your lighting early in the design process; it may impact other decisions to be made regarding the location and type of electrical outlets you need. It was a particular challenge for Ed and Esther because they needed high ceilings to accommodate the large artwork that they prefer. High ceilings can look like deep dark caverns without the proper lighting. The challenge was to create just enough ambient light for the ceiling, while providing accent light for the art. And most of this had to be done from a twenty-foot-high ceiling.

At one point during the building process, Ed and Esther were away for the wedding of a cousin. As the roof went up in the main room, I knew we needed a special fixture for a particular piece of artwork, so I called them on their cell phone. It would add roughly four hundred dollars to our already bulging budget for lights. When I told Esther what I thought we needed, she handed the phone to Ed. I felt like a child asking for more allowance.

It was their decision, but it was my obligation to give them my best advice. The budget was expanded, and they have never regretted that decision. I knew that art was a major part of their lives, and having a clear mission made their decision process easy.

Understanding your own purpose and desires for your home will make your decisions easier too. That way you can focus on what is important to you and not get bogged down with all the trends or what other people think is right for you.

If you buy art, do so because you respond to it on an emotional basis. This means that you are not limited to expensive or investment-level art. Even in Esther and Ed's home, we included their children's artwork and childhood relics as a great way to add emotional satisfaction and spiritual meaning to their home. For example, in the master bedroom, Esther chose to display her childhood gift of an authentic kimono from her uncle's travels to Japan. Obviously, it was no longer something she could wear since it is child-sized. However, she could still enjoy it and remember the significance of this special gift by presenting it as a piece of art. We had it mounted in a Lucite case and hung it above the master bed. Now, every time Esther enters the room, she is reminded of that particular time and the loving relationship she had with her uncle.

Our homes should be reminders of the wonderful times of our lives. I have always believed that the accessories or treasures in our homes should tell the story of our lives. When friends come to visit, our homes should shed some light on who we are and help them to feel like they know us better.

SIMPLICITY MADE SIMPLE

The key to creating a beautiful wall of art is to **CHOOSE SIMILAR SIZES**, styles, or shapes.

Sometimes art is what you see as you look out your window. If you have a wonderful garden, then simply **FRAME YOUR WINDOWS** so that the viewer's eye is drawn outside.

A simple home should reflect the style of all who live there. **HANGING CHILDREN'S ART** is an amazing way to instill confidence and a sense of value in a child.

FIND THE ARTIST IN YOU. If painting is something you have always wanted to do, just do it! I have always wanted to paint, so I did. I actually have one of my first paintings hanging in my dining room.

Photos are art too. **FAMILY PHOTOS** bring a sense of community and are important to a simple home. Designate a wall or two for family photos. Use similar frames and matting for a cohesive look. Remember to update the photos at least every two years to keep things current.

Lord, give me eyes to see what is beautiful
in my life, and gifted hands to display
that beauty so that others can enjoy it too.

PART TWO

Working the Plan

ONCE YOU HAVE a clear understanding of your goals for how you want to live your life, you can arrange your home to fulfill that plan. In this section we explore the tools you will need to express your own personal style. How to light a room, how to choose color, how to arrange furniture, and finally how to make your current home a place for dreams, even if you are still waiting for your dream house.

And There Was Light

And God said, Let there be light: and there was light.

And God saw the light, that it was good:

and God divided the light from the darkness.

And God called the light Day,

and the darkness he called Night. . . .

—GENESIS 1:3–5 (KJV)

God lit the whole world with just His words. As a designer, I only wish lighting rooms were that easy! For us mere humans, it takes a lot of work, wisdom, practice, and patience to accentuate our rooms with effective lighting.

In fact, lighting is probably one of the most complex aspects of decorating. I studied lighting at the General Electric Institute for Lighting, and it still can be a difficult process for me because each situation is different. There is so much to consider. And I have made a few mistakes. The biggest mistake, fortunately for my clients, was in my own home. Here's what happened.

I love decorating what I call pass-through rooms. These are the rooms in our homes that we don't spend time in—we just pass through or use them sparingly, such as the foyer or, as in my case, the powder room. Because we don't spend a lot of time in these rooms, we can punch up the decorating and go a bit beyond our comfort zone, making them more dramatic than we might normally choose. For my powder room, I chose a bold, bright, coral background wallpaper with large-scale white birdcages all over it. The paper is truly beautiful, and I love it. I have a collection of birdhouses in the kitchen, so the birdcages are the perfect complement to this adjoining room.

> ## Lighting is probably one of the most complex aspects of decorating.

I was so excited when the paperhanger began to put it up. The first few sheets were hung and I was thrilled. However, by the time he was finished, something terrible had happened to the color of my paper. It had turned *neon orange*! I mean glaringly orange! Horrible orange. Not nice orange. How could this happen? I had looked at this paper in all different kinds of light and all times of day or night. What was going on?

Well . . . what happened is that, although I had checked the color carefully in the powder room, I had used a three-foot sample length of the paper. And I always left the door to the powder room open when I checked it out. The powder room does not have a window; therefore, there is no natural light in the room. Once the paper was hung, we lost the reflective light of the previously white walls. That white reflection had made up for the lack of natural light (which is white) and allowed the true color of the paper to show.

Now that all the white was covered in coral, the softening effect of the white walls was eliminated. The problem was compounded by the fact that to actually use the powder room for its intended purpose, you must *close* the door—preventing any natural light from streaming into the room. As a result, what was once a pretty coral color was now something that required sunglasses to look at. Even changing lightbulbs to full-spectrum natural light did not help.

You may be wondering why I have not fixed this problem. Actually, I am not sure. I do know that I have never made that mistake again. But as a designer, I am my own worst client. The problem is that because of my work I can't stop shopping after I have made a choice. Instead, I continue to see all the new and beautiful papers that are released each year. So, as a result, I am *extremely careful* in choosing my own items to ensure that I will not be disappointed when I see next season's new products. I tell you this so you know that mine was not a hasty decision.

Just recently I had to face the music of this past mistake again when friends came to visit from Tennessee. They still seem to enjoy laughing about my bright orange room—and laugh we did. Their teenagers who have known me since they were toddlers laughed the loudest. The fact is, I still love the paper and am hoping to discover a solution sometime in the future. Perhaps I should just hang a pair of sunglasses on the outside doorknob with a sign recommending: "Wearing sunglasses before entering this room is advised for your safety and protection!"

This just proves that God's light is the best. There is nothing like the beauty of natural light to bring out the best in all things.

> There is nothing like the beauty of natural light to bring out the best in all things.

SIMPLE TRUTH ABOUT LIGHT

As illustrated in my orange powder room, lighting can make or break a color design. Choosing a variety of lighting sources can go a long way toward creating the perfect ambiance for just the mood you want when you want it. The key to a well-lit room is the ability to change the mood of the room depending on the time of day or how you want to use the room. A warm and welcoming lighting system consists of these three basic types of lighting: ambient, accent, and task.

Ambient light provides the greatest diffusion of light. It fills the space with soft illumination. Ambient fixtures can be ceiling-mounted styles such as recessed cans or fluorescent fixtures. Or they may be wall-mounted lamps that project lighting upward toward the ceiling. I prefer to use a dimmer for ambient light so that one can control the mood simply by adjusting the level of light in the room. All of the rooms in my house have ceiling fixtures because they provide abundant light for cleaning and can be dimmed for a soft mood.

Accent fixtures (sometimes called focus lighting) are usually chandeliers, pendants, or other decorative lamps. Accent lights are often used to add extra light or focus on a specific area. It is often directional lighting, which is used to create emphasis on objects or artwork. The most effective accent lighting will direct your eye to specific items or architectural features within a room. It also has the ability to create the illusion of a larger space when it is focused on the perimeter of the room. Think about how your eye is drawn to the light of a window—even a small room feels bigger with the light streaming in through the window. A similar effect can be accomplished by highlighting the far wall of a small room with light.

The height of your ceiling directly influences the proper placement of focus lighting. Most adjustable down lights (recessed ceiling fixtures) have a maximum tilt of thirty-five degrees. This means you will need to do some calculations to determine the best placement of your fixture to most effectively light wall-hung objects. For example, if you have an eight-foot-high ceiling, then your fixture should be

> The most effective accent lighting will direct your eye to specific items or architectural features within a room.

placed twenty inches from the wall for average eye-level viewing (sixty-three inches from the floor). If your ceiling is nine feet high, place the fixture twenty-seven inches from the wall for best eye-level viewing. A ten-foot ceiling requires the fixture to be placed thirty-three inches from the wall.

The taller ceilings are the most difficult for eye-level viewing. A room with a ceiling of twelve feet or more requires that the accent light be placed approximately seventy-five inches from the wall. At that distance, however, the light can be so diffused that it does not accomplish what you had hoped for. There are more expensive fixtures that are specifically designed for lighting art in this situation. They almost all use halogen lamps.

Task lighting is just what it sounds like—light that makes it easier to see the task at hand. It can be a reading lamp beside your favorite chair, or it can be a recessed light strategically placed above your kitchen counter or workstation. To avoid casting your own shadow, install task lights slightly in front of and above the surface where you will be working.

There are also three basic types of bulbs (technically called lamps): incandescent, halogen, and fluorescent. Each provides a specific color of light and cost of energy.

SIMPLICITY MADE SIMPLE

CHOOSE a halogen bulb which can be dimmed for dining as a brighter light for cooking.

TO GIVE A ROOM SOFTER LIGHT without darkening the space, consider a pastel incandescent bulb. Choose a pink or peach color to give your room a happy glow.

THE BEST LIGHT for making the most of your makeup is still the Hollywood-style vanity fixture. They use a ball-shaped lamp, which creates fewer shadows on your face when mounted above your mirror on the wall. Be sure to use the translucent rather than the clear bulbs. I recommend no more than a twenty-five-watt lamp so that you won't need sunglasses to put on your eye shadow.

Halogen lamps provide a brighter, whiter light. They are **IDEAL FOR READING** because they are small and can be positioned directly on what you are reading or working on. They are generally more expensive but will last up to two years.

If you are looking for a lamp that is **CLOSEST TO NATURAL LIGHT**, try one of the newer, full-spectrum styles. The Reveal bulb, which is made by General Electric, filters the yellow light of the standard lamp, making colors more vivid and less washed out.

Lord, thank You for promising
to light my life with Your Word.
Continue to guide me in the way
that I should go, and cause the way I live
to shine as a beacon to others who are looking
for a way out of darkness.

Color—the Most Powerful Decorating Tool

With the color that paints the morning
and the evening clouds that face the sun
I saw then the whole heaven suffused.

—DANTE ALIGHIERI (1265–1321)

As has been well documented, color stirs the senses. I've seen people react physically and emotionally to the colors around them. Research has shown that red makes our hearts beat faster. Blue is calming, yellow enhances concentration, and green refreshes. The effects of bold, dramatic color are far-reaching and they cannot be ignored. Color can motivate, de-stress, improve one's disposition, and even help control appetite. So why are so many people afraid of choosing or using it in their decorating?

The trouble is that some people aren't even sure which colors they like. Others fear that bright, colorful rooms may be thought of as childish, unsophisticated, Bohemian, too trendy—or worse, not trendy enough. Others say they're overwhelmed by all the choices. In interior design, as in art, harmony comes from a pleasing arrangement of colors.

Our response to color is influenced first by our ability to see color. My personal color theory is that the world is divided into two kinds of people—people who prefer green tones and people who prefer blue tones. I have spent thirty years refining this theory and have been able to document it scientifically. Blue and green are the two colors to which we have the strongest response. Not a surprise; I believe it is God's design. Just staring at green grass has been shown to reduce blood pressure. And there is nothing more beautiful than an awesome God-colored blue sky.

Let color inspire you!

Did you know that the majority of color-blind people are men? It's true. As a result, many men do not even see the color green; it appears gray to them. Those men who are not color-blind are often green people because they have the ability to see it. They also often turn out to be extremely creative because their ability to see many colors is stimulating to their creative side.

The Dakota Indians of Minnesota have the same word for both blue and green. *To* means blue or green. *Pezi To* is green, and *Mahpiya To* is blue. I found this interesting. Obviously, they too saw the significance of these two colors.

I am fortunate because God gave me an innately strong sense of color. I wait with anticipation for the day when I get to heaven and will be able to see colors that I cannot even imagine now. The colors that surround God's throne are described in Revelation 4:2–3, 6 (NIV): "At once I was in the Spirit, and there before me was a throne in heaven with someone sitting on it. And the one who sat there had the appearance of jasper and carnelian. A rainbow, resembling an emerald, encircled the throne. . . . Also before the throne there was what looked like a sea of glass, clear as crystal."

A green person, of whom I am one, can be irritated by certain colors of blue. Understanding our own response to color can give us the ability to use color to positively influence our lives—both physically and emotionally. Because of the associations we have with colors that appear in nature, some are considered cool (green grass, blue water). Others are warm (red fire, yellow sun). Did you know that all colors contain *other* colors? For example, red may have a blue or an orange base.

Paint is the least expensive way to give your home a big boost. In selecting colors for your home, you should begin with colors you like—colors that make you smile. To begin composing a color scheme, I recommend working from the color palette of something you love. It can be a scarf, painting, carpet, wallpaper, or anything that uses colors that make you feel good. From this choose your three main colors.

As you develop your color scheme, consider its color *value*, which is the relative lightness or darkness of a color. Never mix a dark-valued color with a light-valued color. For example, a pale peach just doesn't seem right with a strong green. The weights of the colors are too different. Instead use pale colors with pale and strong with strong. Adding black makes a change in *shade*; and a *tint* is a color with white added. The green chintz you think might be a perfect match for your walls can feel all wrong because the shade has too much of another color, like yellow, in it.

> Paint is the least expensive way to give your home a big boost.

In working with one of my clients, we discovered that she was drawn to purple. I don't mean pretty pale lavender. I mean purple in all its bold glory. She even asked if we could paint the entire first floor of her new townhouse purple.

I began to analyze the living space. The open floor plan of her home meant that only one room, the dining room, actually had four walls. One wall had a beautiful big window, and two walls had large openings to other rooms. The fourth wall had a large breakfront cabinet placed against it.

After gaining confidence that my client could actually handle living with the bold shade of purple, we decided to go for it. We even painted the ceiling in the dining room purple. We used fresh bright white for the trim, which complemented our base color.

As the painters began the process of applying this color, my client was certain they would respond with shock. Instead, they loved it. The stunning purple was the perfect background for this client's Southern formal style of decorating. It feels traditional yet exciting. Everyone was amazed at her bold choice, and because they loved it, they even seemed to envy her courage!

SURROUND YOURSELF WITH COLOR

When considering color, don't stop at the walls. A colorful floor is a simple way to transform a room. You can choose a vibrant area rug, tiles, carpet, or even colorful stenciling to conceal worn-out hardwood. Covering a floor with a colorful kilim, a bright, multicolored flat weave rug, is a simple way to add drama to a space. If you tire of it, all you have to do is roll it up and put it away.

> Add a dramatic flair with whimsical touches and glorious colors.

Furnishings, both upholstered pieces and case goods (various types of cabinetry, chests, desks, bedsteads, tables, and chairs), can make a color statement too. For example, I used simple, red lacquered chairs in my kitchen to pump up the energy and complement my natural pine farm table.

Window treatments give you lots of flexibility. I worked with someone who was very reluctant to try anything outside of the neutral color palette she had chosen for her living room. So we kept the wall color soft, adding just enough color to highlight the woodwork and architectural details. Then we chose a golden plaid fabric for the drapes, which added color in a subtle way.

Accessories are ideal for pulling colors together in a room. You can use pillows, throws, table runners, artwork, floral arrangements—anything that pleases you, and as many or as few pieces as you like.

In my experience, I've come to think of color as a relatively inexpensive tool that can change the way you feel about your rooms. By painting, papering, or adding pillows to the mix, you can create a new mood, enhance a space, and liven up your home without extensive architectural changes.

Did you ever wonder how colors become popular? There is a business council that predetermines the colors for each year. When I first learned of this, I was a bit miffed that the color choices for different products would always be limited in some way. But the reality is that if someone weren't coordinating all the different facets of both fashion design and interior design, then it would be nearly impossible to find anything that matched.

Recently, there has been a lot of focus by practicing designers on using colors that induce a sense of hope, such as strong bluish pink, happy yellows, geranium reds, and warm orange. They have found that people consistently respond to certain colors emotionally, and are drawn to colors that give them hope. With the state of the world today, we all need hope. The obvious hope is faith in God. But God did create color and its emotional effect; therefore, why not use colors that evoke hope on a physical level to give us a boost?

Use color to visually bridge together your furnishings and accessories while setting a comfortable mood that revives you and your guests.

SIMPLICITY MADE SIMPLE

REMEMBER that paint always looks stronger on walls than it does on paint chips. What appears subtle on paper may be a bit too much on your walls, so choose your shades wisely.

When using two different colors in adjoining rooms, **USE THE SAME TRIM COLOR** throughout to visually unite the rooms.

Because the same color will appear darker on the ceiling than it does on the wall, **TINT THE CEILING COLOR** a bit by adding white.

DO A "BRUSH-OUT" FIRST. Paint your color on a large sheet of illustration board or foam core and then look at it in your room. Be sure to move it from wall to wall.

REMEMBER that light affects our impression of color, so check your choice in natural light (both morning and afternoon) as well as incandescent light.

EVEN THINGS OUT. Be sure your color choices share the same level of intensity (the relative purity or brightness of a color) from room to room. Intense colors are vivid and fresh, while low-intensity colors are more understated.

Lord, as I look at the world around me, I am in awe
of the colors displayed in Your handiwork.
And as I read Your Word, I am reminded that
You have promised peace to Your people (Psalm 85:8).
Help me to reflect Your peace in my home.

Putting Together a Plan
for Living

A good plan is like a road map:

it shows the final destination

and usually the best way to get there.

—H. STANLEY JUDD, *THINK RICH*

Before I attended design school, I thought of myself as a creative person. But during my education, I felt I was losing my sense of artistic expression. There were so many rules and regulations regarding design that I felt as though I no longer had the freedom to express unique ideas. I spoke with one of my professors about my frustration and told him how dismayed I felt. He gave me back my freedom of creative expression by explaining that once I knew the rules, I was allowed to break them.

That simple statement made all the difference for me. So I am giving you that same freedom for your home. The principles I share here will assist you in simplifying a plan for your home, but remember they are only guidelines, not unbreakable rules. After all, this is your home and your life. What matters the most is finding a plan that makes sense for you and your family and the way you want to live.

If, for you, having a simple home means filling it to the brim with lovingly placed treasures, then so be it. Too often, we allow what others may think to influence us to the point that it is no longer our personality or life that is reflected in our own spaces.

SIMPLE KEYS TO FURNITURE ARRANGEMENT

Small rooms, in particular, can be the most special little treasures. Having a good floor plan is key to all rooms, but it is especially critical for small spaces. The key to a good floor plan is balance. Balance has two dimensions: *physical balance* and *optical balance*. In other words, you want to be sure that the arrangement of high and low furniture, combined with the high and low architectural elements (windows, doors, fireplace, etc.), is balanced.

> What matters the most is to find a plan that makes sense for you and your family.

For example, if you have a fireplace centered on the wall with a window to the right side, it would make good balance sense to place something of similar height and size to the window on the left side of the fireplace. An item such as a tall mirror or a tall bookcase to the left of the fireplace gives the wall optical balance. An example of physical balance would be to place two chairs opposite each other that are equal in physical proportion, including the footprint (amount of floor space required) and weight of each.

To begin arranging your room, you need a floor plan from which to work. Start by measuring your space and laying it out to scale on graph paper or try one of the many home-improvement or furniture Web sites that have room planners on them.

I still prefer the old-fashioned paper-and-pencil method, where one-quarter inch is equal to one foot. I just think, this way, that I have more control over the process. With computerized planners, I find I spend more time trying to make the room fit into some programmed system rather than being creative about the process.

Once you have drawn your basic room to scale showing windows, doorways, and other built-in features, determine the major focal point. A focal point should be the thing that draws your eye to itself. Sometimes this is an obvious architectural element such as a fireplace. Other times it will be necessary to create a focal point by the way you arrange your furniture. A wall system, conversation area, or even a game table can be the focus of a room. In a bedroom, particularly the master bedroom, the bed should always be the focal point, even if there is a strong architectural element such as a fireplace.

The key to a good floor plan is balance.

Once the focal point is established, continue by placing the furniture into the space starting with the largest items. This is because there is usually limited space in which the large items actually fit. The remaining pieces of furniture should be placed according to their respective sizes with the smallest pieces being placed last.

Most floor plans are either symmetrical or asymmetrical, which means, for example, either you are placing sofas opposite each other, or you are not. Formal period rooms are always symmetrical. Asymmetrical design is more casual and more flexible.

If you have a small room, you may want to consider placing the sofa on the diagonal across a corner with the rest of the pieces placed in a working relationship to it. By placing furniture on the diagonal angle, you create the illusion of more space. The angle fools the eye.

One of my clients had a small living room that was hardly used by anyone. By simply making a floor-plan change with the sofa placed on the diagonal angle and arranging the rest of the furniture around it, we had nearly instantaneous results from her children. The very next day, without prompting, her children gravitated to the room. When she came in after school, she found all three of them sitting in the living room and reading. Two weeks later, when I visited them, I too saw the same results: Her three children were sitting and reading, perfectly content, in the newly arranged living room.

So the question is *Why?* What made the difference that drew the children to this previously unused room? I think it was simply more inviting. It *felt* good, and getting a positive response from your family is the goal of a simple home. You want your home to inspire good feelings on an emotional level, meet the family's needs, and be easy to care for.

BE CREATIVE WITH SMALL SPACES

One of the biggest mistakes most people make in small rooms is believing they must use small-scale furniture and small-scale patterns. Often, just the opposite is true. Proportion is critical to a well-balanced room, but large rooms are often more problematic than small ones because the furniture can feel dwarfed by soaring vaulted ceilings. However, in a small room a few larger-scale pieces can give the illusion of a bigger space.

One of my clients had a tiny living room that she hoped could be a cozy den. We started by creating a focal point with a large oil painting placed in the center of the back wall. We then added two larger-scale overstuffed chairs in a pretty blue with matching ottomans, and a thirty-inch-round table between them. The only window in the room was dressed with a soft, silky balloon shade with tight sheers beneath. The sheer provided privacy while still allowing light to filter into the room, and the balloon shade added a feminine touch to the space. A softly hued, flat-weave rug with a floral center medallion finished the room along with a few well-placed large-scale accessories. The overall effect was beautiful, and you didn't even notice the small size of the space.

In fact, even the delivery men were surprised. Their first comment to me was that the chairs were never going to fit in this room! Then they were amazed at the transformation and how the large-scaled items not only fit but also created a visual illusion of abundant space. If I had chosen to use several pieces of small-scale furniture, it would have chopped the room into many small items. The key was using a *few* larger-sized pieces and keeping everything in proportion to them, including the large oil painting on the wall.

SIMPLICITY MADE SIMPLE

PLAN FOR EASY TRAFFIC FLOW. Be sure to provide walkways with a minimum of twenty-eight inches. If you are really tight on space, you can get away with twenty inches. This may feel small on paper, but in reality, most furniture within a room is below eye level. Therefore, you need less room when there is nothing obstructing your view.

If you want your family to spend more time conversing with one another, then be sure to **ARRANGE CONVERSATION AREAS** within your living spaces. Seating should be close enough for easy communication without causing a "Mom-he's-in-my-space-again" argument.

BE AWARE of too many legs in one room. This time I am talking about table and chair legs, not kids. Too many pieces of furniture with tall legs can leave a room feeling a bit off balance.

Many people struggle with **HOW TO FILL EMPTY CORNERS**. Here are a few ideas: tall display or curio cabinets, a large plant, a decorative screen, or even an arrangement of several pieces of artwork placed on the adjacent walls can beautifully fill an empty corner.

To give the illusion of a taller ceiling, **KEEP THE EYE MOVING UPWARD** by adding architectural details like crown molding or simply placing taller artwork within the space.

AVOID placing several tall pieces of furniture together. Instead, provide variation by using lower horizontal items between them.

If you have a large room, **TRY DIVIDING IT UP** into distinct areas for specific tasks such as reading, music, or television watching. Use small rugs to help define each area and provide a foundation.

> Father, bless my home to be a place
> that nurtures those who share these walls.
> Show me creative ways to encourage people
> to share life together here.

Defining by Design

The contented man is never poor;
the discontented man is never rich.

—GEORGE ELIOT (1819–1880)

From a biblical perspective the above quotation could be translated: "Be content with what you have" (Hebrews 13:5, NIV). The word *contentment* comes from the Greek verb *arkeo*, which means "be enough, be sufficient." This conveys a sense of freedom from reliance on other people or things. Being content is often easier if we are also patient. Having patience regarding your home projects can go a long way in helping you enjoy what you have now.

Thinking creatively can be an invaluable asset in giving your home a fresh perspective and new life. When I first visit a home or homesite, I spend time just quietly allowing my senses to see and hear the home and its surroundings. My work is to design inhabited space; therefore I must first consider the real values of how people will relate to each other in the space that I am designing. It is understanding who my clients are, what they enjoy doing, and how they want to spend their time that allows me to creatively connect design to their lives.

To accomplish this goal of blending design with functional interpersonal activities, I find it critical that I emotionally connect with the space. I need to know where the natural light is and how I can best make use of it. I explore the good and bad architectural features so I can use or minimize them. I consider ways in which I can create balance in the space. And I take lots of photos, measure everything, and allow my mind to envision possibilities of real life taking place in this space. Nothing concrete—just a playful imagination running wild. I consider how I would use the space if I lived there. For the moment, I forget the rules and just allow myself the freedom to enjoy and experience the possibilities of the space. It is those first, almost childlike emotions that I hang on to when I work on a floor plan. I trust my instincts and responses to the space.

After I have a clear picture of how I think the space could best be used, I involve the family by asking questions, lots of questions, regarding how they want to live and how that differs from how they *are* living. I encourage you to try experimenting with this idea yourself.

For example, if you and your family would like to consider taking music lessons, then think about how you can change your spaces to best accommodate the idea. Perhaps you love to play board games, but it's too much work to clear the dining room table to make room for such fun. Then consider adding a game table to your family room. Maybe you never use your dining room for formal entertaining. Consider how it can be used to make more sense for your lifestyle. Make notes about how you would like to use a space, then ask family members for their ideas.

Experiencing the life you want is a key issue for learning to love your home, because often it is not the house that leaves you feeling short of your goals, but it is the choices you have made within it that cause you disappointment. As Jim Tolpin, author of *The New Family Home*, says, "A home is a place to bring everyone together, not to send them off to their rooms. Today's home strives to be the most important place to everybody in the family. But to be such a place, it must really work for the people who call it home."

For most busy families, this could mean providing a space for hulking teenagers to hang out as well as a sanctuary retreat for mom and dad. A study by the building industry a few years ago provided what I think is essential for creating the perfect family home. They polled family members of all ages, from four to one hundred and four. And they all wanted the same thing from a home: a place for families to come together and a place where they could individually go off to be alone. I believe that God hardwired us with both of these needs. Since the home is the only environment over which we have sustained control, it is the only place to truly provide for both these needs.

As I often tell my clients, much to their dismay, a home is never finished, because the people living in it are continuously growing and changing. The key to a simple family-friendly home is creating one that is designed for change, with rooms that can be used for different functions. This means planning rooms and spaces that can do double duty now and be rearranged for a new purpose later. For example, a home office can double as a guest room now. And later it may be a bedroom for an aging parent.

> A home is never finished, because the people living in it are continuously growing and changing.

TAKE A BUYER'S LOOK AT YOUR HOME

One suggestion that may help you to see your home anew is to pretend you are seeing it for the first time. I know this will be difficult, but try it. On paper, list the things that you perceive to be the positive and negative attributes of your home. What are the things you absolutely love about your home? Too often, we get stuck focusing on what we do not like rather than on what we do like about our homes.

Pretend again that you are selling your home, and write an advertisement for its sale. You would certainly highlight all the good and wonderful attributes, wouldn't you? Perhaps there are great architectural details. If not, they can always be added, so make a list of what you would improve.

I live in a home that is ten years old. It did not have a lot of extra details when I built it. The fact is, I could not afford them. But over the years, I have slowly been adding the details I like. You would be amazed at the transformation in my master bathroom. I changed what was a carpeted floor to beautiful tiles. I replaced the faucets and towel bars with brass fixtures. I added simple stock molding from a home improvement store around the mirror above the vanity table. In addition, I papered the walls and around the ceiling I added crown molding from a home store. The crown molding and the framing around the mirror made a significant difference. Those simple details brought the room to a whole new level. Friends have even asked where I found my huge mirror. It's still the inexpensive mirror that was glue-mounted on the wall originally. I simply added the molding and painted it.

Many people have homes that they dislike because they have rooms that are too small. This is especially true of the 1950s bungalows and the 1960s Colonials. There is often sufficient square footage, but it's just too chopped up to make sense for today's way of living. One of the biggest lessons I learned while working with an architect on my own home was to eliminate hallways and expand the rooms into them—and then expand the opening to each room to six or eight feet. The wider openings will make smaller areas feel larger while still providing delineation of space. With some basic interior changes, your rooms will feel more connected, which is more conducive to family being together. Another way to create a more open and spacious feeling is to use half-walls that set boundaries without blocking the view.

> Pretend that you are selling your home, and write a For Sale ad.

If remodeling is an option, cozy spaces can be made to feel larger by adding additional or larger windows. Perhaps you have seen the magazine ad that encourages you to *imagine* the difference a larger window can make? Not that I believe everything I read or see in an advertisement, but it is amazing how an expanded view can change a room. Even interior windows such as transoms over doorways (with or without doors) can provide a feeling of openness while still giving a sense of definition.

For one of my clients, we converted the dining room into a library/home office. We added wood-carved doors to close off the opening to the foyer, with transoms above to allow light from the foyer to stream in. Then we closed the opening from the kitchen with French glass-paned doors. That way he still can feel connected to the family in the kitchen, while having peace and quiet to work. It also gives his young children a sense of security knowing and seeing that Daddy is near.

SIMPLICITY MADE SIMPLE

A CHANGE IN FLOORING easily designates spaces within a large area. Something as simple as adding an area rug under a dining table or in a conversation area defines a smaller area beautifully.

A RELATIVELY INEXPENSIVE WAY to add space and light to a room is to add a bumped-out alcove. It immediately changes the space. It is perfect for a kitchen table and chairs or for a built-in window seat with storage below.

TRY RAISING THE ROOF to add volume to a room. This is probably the most dramatic change you can make. Kitchens, family rooms, and even master bedrooms can benefit from this remodeling project.

Sometimes, **LOWERING THE CEILING LINE** is what makes the most sense. A ceiling that is lowered over a specific area, such as a dining area, will define and make it special.

ALLOW YOURSELF TO DREAM—if someone gave you several thousand dollars to spend on your home, how would you spend it? You are not allowed to move. And you cannot go over budget. This is a great way to help you begin to figure out how to make your home work for you.

USE YOUR NOOKS and crannies. It is amazing what you can do with them. One of my favorites is building bookcases into them, or creating a special homework area there.

ADD windows and skylights to tall walls and ceilings to bring in additional natural light.

If you have a room that is just too long, divide it by adding a glass-paned French door to **CREATE TWO ROOMS**. Or you can use furniture to optically divide a space. For example, place your sofa in the middle of the room. This can designate the change in space. The placement of a carpet can accomplish the same distinction.

> Lord, I thank You for my home and for showing me
> how to live the quality of life I long to enjoy.
> I know that the good life does not require
> that my home look a certain way.
> I am content, and because I am made
> in Your image I am also creative. Help me
> to make the most with what You have given me.

Can You Love
the Home You Have?

Thou shalt rejoice in every good thing
which the Lord thy God hath given unto thee,
and unto thine house. . . .

—DEUTERONOMY 26:11 (KJV)

When I am working with first-time homebuyers, I often find myself reminding them that this is not their dream home—but a step toward their dream home. However, through my years of practice as an interior designer and a licensed real estate agent, I have found that sometimes what begins as a starter home can become a forever home. That does not mean that it suddenly became a dream home. It just means that somewhere along the way, the starter home became filled with love, family, cherished memories, and, last but not least, a paid-in-full mortgage. It's amazing what a little time and an attitude change can do for a home.

But what if time has not brought a change in how you feel about your home?

What if you really don't like what you have? Life is full of unexpected twists and turns. Plan as we may, sometimes we fall victim to the plans of fate. I went through a divorce after twenty years of marriage. I didn't plan it. I didn't even know it was coming. Nonetheless, it happened. Part of the divorce process was that a home had to be sold and equity divided.

Unfortunately, the tax laws were not changed in time for me to benefit from the one-time tax exemption rule. I was faced with either buying a new house immediately or paying an exorbitant amount of capital gains tax, so I decided to build a house. And because of the tax laws, it made the most sense to purchase a larger home than I would have under today's tax law. I complicated my situation by building a house that I thought I could resell easily, rather than building a house suited to me. I never planned on living here for any length of time. In fact, I wasn't even sure I was going to stay in Pennsylvania because I had no family ties here. I thought I was only staying long enough to recover emotionally with the help of my support group that was here. In addition, my clientele was here and that's how I was supporting myself. And finally, looking for a new job while I was trying to recover from a divorce was just not something I was willing to try.

> It's amazing what a little time and an attitude change can do for a home.

Please don't misunderstand, the house is very nice. I made sure it had the features that I thought would be most desirable to a homebuyer. Now ten years later, I am still in this house. I married a local guy, and he moved in too. The problem is, this is not my heart-home. As I said, I built this house for someone else to live in, not for me.

If I had built a home for me it would have been a cute little French cottage—preferably near the water somewhere. Instead, I am in a well-kept development of houses that many have coined "McMansions." Trust me, my home is not a McMansion. It is the smallest house in this suburban community. It is a one-and-a-half-story home with a finished daylight/walkout basement. The basement has a family room, kitchenette, office/guest room, full bath, and two storage areas. We have a first-floor master bedroom, and a beautiful high vaulted ceiling in the main room.

So what is my problem? My problem is that it is more house than *I* want. I wish it were cozy with lots of details. I wish it had a better quality kitchen. Mine is a stock kitchen with resilient flooring. I would prefer a wood floor and Zodiac countertops (a combination of quartz and resins). However, this home has served us well.

Eventually, I sold the downtown building that housed my design studio, and I moved my work into the basement guest room. Then my husband Dave moved his business into the house. With his business came computers, copiers, files, and desks, along with help. All of this conveniently fit into the finished basement.

A HOUSE FOR DREAMS IS BETTER THAN A DREAM HOME

Charles Spurgeon, one of England's best-known preachers (1834–1892), wrote, "It is not how much we have but how much we enjoy." I think his statement comments on how contentment is a matter of attitude and gratitude toward those things that God has provided.

If my home were a little cottage, none of the changes would have been possible. So I have accepted that this is the best place to be. Last year when I was sure it was time to move because I had found an amazing little carriage house, Dave panicked. Just the thought of moving nearly put him over the edge. When I prayed about it, God said, "Wait." So I waited. And then unexpectedly, I got another contract to write a series of books. Now I too have a helper working at the house with me. This would never have been possible if we had moved to the little cottage I thought was my dream house.

And over time, I have made the most of this home. Yes, it is now my *home*. When I received my first book contract I built a screened-in porch. Dave and I love our porch, and now we would not want a home without one. I have personalized my kitchen with a hand-painted mural of a tree filled with birdhouses. It stretches up into the vaulted area above the kitchen table. I love it! I even ordered some badly needed furniture for the bedroom.

> By working to make your home a reflection of you, you make it a better home.

I have added to the landscaping bit by bit, year by year. I planted three elm trees four years ago. They now envelop the porch, providing privacy and shade. I am proud of my trees. I feel good about the plants and flowers, the little round patio made of pavers, and especially the lavender plants, fresh or dried, that give me a year-round peaceful aroma for calming my often overstimulated state of mind.

I am making a commitment to this home one step at a time. And as I do, I am learning to love it more each step of the way. It doesn't mean that I have given up on the dream of a little cottage. It just means that for today this is where I am, which must mean this is where God wants me. And that simply translates to this is where *I belong*.

Sometimes a home is for a season. And seasons change. But in the meantime, just as with all of life, we must learn to make the most of it. Just as we wear warm clothes in winter, we must also dress our homes for the seasons that we live in them.

SIMPLICITY MADE SIMPLE

DEVELOP AN ATTITUDE OF THANKFULNESS while allowing God to work out the plans He has for you. We all know that even if we don't feel thankful, we can act as if we do. And often, our heart will follow our behavior.

Despite what the real estate agents tell you, **MAKE YOUR HOME YOUR OWN**. Make it work for how you want to live, not for its resale appeal. In most cases, the new owners are going to tear out whatever you do—including the newly remodeled bathroom—because they want a shower and not a whirlpool tub.

ENLIST THE HELP of your best friend—ask her to tell you what she loves most about your home. This can help you learn to appreciate your home in new ways.

Don't tackle your entire house at once. You will end up with many unfinished rooms. Instead, **TRY MINI WEEKEND-LONG PROJECTS**. Start with whatever bothers you most about your home. Remember, something as simple as a new paint color can make a room a place you enjoy.

ACCESSORIES can be all you need to make your home more lovable. By choosing a theme for your decorating, you can easily purchase accessories to carry that theme throughout your home. For example, give your home a charming character with old-world-style accessories such as a floral painted plate on an elegant stand, or a pair of fanciful burgundy and gold buffet lamps with striped shades trimmed in fringe.

REARRANGE your furniture—it's my mother's favorite thing to do. Too often, we get stuck in thinking furniture has to stay in the room it is in—just because it's there. Instead, try redecorating by moving select pieces from one room to another. Consider redoing your most-used room by borrowing things from other rooms. You will be amazed at the difference it can make.

If you like to change your rooms around a lot, or you are always changing your mind about colors, then **KEEP A NEUTRAL PALETTE** in the background (walls, floors, etc.) so you can easily restyle things whenever you want.

Thank You, Lord, for giving me what I need even before I realize I will need it. You alone know tomorrow's secret, and I am grateful that I can simply put my trust in You to take care of all my needs.

PART THREE

Adapting to Real Life

THE MOST IMPORTANT STEP in making a home is learning to enjoy what you have. I encourage you to trust your instincts when it comes to making final choices for decorating your house. Real life is a matter of enjoying the people around you, and I will show you how that is easier to do in spaces that appeal to your senses and soul.

Making Your Home Your Own

Efficiency and convenience alone don't bring joy;
beauty is the mysterious element.

—ALEXANDRA STODDARD, *CREATING A BEAUTIFUL HOME*

The term *simple* often gets confused with *sparse*. They can be the same thing, but it is not necessary to be bare or sparse to make a home simple. It can be *simply* beautiful. And beautiful can simply mean that something is good—that it makes us happy.

In Luke 21:1–6 (NAS), Jesus was in the temple with His disciples when He pointed to a widow who had given *all that she had* to the temple treasury. He was trying to tell the disciples she had done a good and beautiful thing, but it seems that the disciples weren't even listening to what He was saying. Instead of responding to His comment, they pointed out the beautiful stones and votive gifts in the temple.

Jesus said, "As for these things which you are looking at, the days will come in which there will not be left one stone upon another which will not be torn down." I believe Jesus was making many points here, but one of them was to show us that what the disciples saw as beautiful was only temporal. What Jesus saw as beautiful was the good heart of the widow woman. *She made Him happy.*

I believe that it is this kind of thing or person that Paul suggested when he wrote, "Finally, brothers, whatever is true, whatever is noble, whatever is right, whatever is pure, whatever is lovely, whatever is admirable—if anything is excellent or praiseworthy—think about such things" (Philippians 4:8, NIV). There is no better way to describe beauty, in my mind, than this Scripture.

Beauty is focusing on the acts of love within our homes, rather than the beautiful gifts that adorn our homes. This is the beauty that will bring lasting happiness to us. Decorating our walls with beautiful objects won't make us love our homes. We must learn to focus on the good that happens therein. But as in the temple, both the walls and the activities in our home can be beautiful.

GOD GAVE EACH OF US OUR OWN STYLE

In nature, God set the standard for beauty. Every night He paints a new sunset for us to enjoy, and every morning a new sunrise. He uses color and light to create moods conducive to our pleasure. We can agree that beauty was God's idea, and He has given each of us our own sense of style. Our homes can reflect all the good aspects of His creative presence in our lives.

As a designer, I am inspired to do my most excellent work in making a home beautiful for the people who ask for my help. I am often asked what is my signature design style. I find it a hard question to answer because I never design a client's home for *my style*. My work is to discover an individual's God-given style and help reveal what appeals to him or her.

I know that many designers, especially the celebrity designers, have a very specific style for which they are known—which is great, but it means they only attract people who want that look. I always encourage my clients to discover their own style.

Once, when I was being interviewed for an article on designer styles, I asked several of my clients what they thought my style was. They confirmed that I did not have one unique style but worked to make them happy. My challenge of helping each person express his or her uniqueness makes each project more interesting. More important, working to help others express their own tastes makes me a better designer.

> Our homes can reflect all aspects of God's creative presence in our lives.

WHERE IS YOUR HAPPY PLACE?

One question I ask my clients is, "What is your favorite room in the house?" I ask this question because it immediately transports them to a *happy place*. If you saw the movie *Happy Gilmore*, then you know what I am talking about. In the movie, the golf therapist suggests to the golfer that before he takes a swing, he should imagine himself in his happy place. When I ask my clients about their happy room, it's amazing how the expression on their faces changes to a smile. They suddenly become more animated—even joyful.

So I ask you, "What is it about your favorite room that makes you happy?" Is it the sun streaming through the windows? Is it the comfortable chair in the corner with your grandmother's afghan? Knowing what makes you happy about that space is critical to making the rest of your home more special.

Perhaps your favorite room existed in another home, or even at your childhood home. Sometimes there is an emotional response to a time and place, and not necessarily any one specific style or item about a room that makes you happy. After all, allowing yourself to think back on where you were when a good time happened can easily trigger happy memories from your childhood. That too can give you insight into how to decorate your home.

If you use a style or an item in your decorating scheme that transports you emotionally to some happy memory, you will always enjoy being in that room or space. (Women, in particular, often share happy memories that morph into romantic ideals.) If the blissful memory happened when you were young and giddy, and you got excited about flowers, lace, and other frilly things, then a room decorated in such a way would transport you to that joyful time. This may translate into a romantic decorating style that can be incorporated throughout your home. That doesn't mean you make it uncomfortable for everyone else. You can create a simple romantic look without making it too froufrou.

> Happy memories can give you insight into how to decorate your home.

For example, some men would cringe if I started hanging fringed scarves on the windows and lace coverlets on the bed. It's just too frilly! But by combining awning-style stripes with a delicate floral twill fabric in a faded rose color you can create a quietly luminous yet welcoming style that won't scare the guys in your family. (Hmmm . . . maybe you do want to scare them from a room—that way you get a room of your own!)

Speaking of guys . . . I am often asked how guys feel about decorating. Do they care? If so, about what? Do they care about the master bedroom? Do they care about the kitchen? I find that, just like with women, it varies from guy to guy. Yes, some men don't care as long as their wives are within budget and happy. But some men *pretend* not to care because they don't think anyone will listen. Other times they are hesitant to express themselves because they don't think they know enough to do it right, and they feel inadequate.

As I work with clients, I make it very clear from the beginning that I want both partners involved. I want all family members to express themselves and have a place within the home to call their own. In the end, they enjoy seeing how the process of design develops. And when they are allowed to participate and understand the significance of the work, it can make life easier and better for the entire family. When husbands are involved with the process, they are less likely to balk.

QUALITY (THAT WHICH IS GOOD) HAS A PRICE

The key to budgeting is understanding what you get for your money. In my work experience, I've realized that since most people only decorate, renovate, or purchase home furnishings two to three times in a lifetime, they usually experience sticker shock. They have no idea why things cost what they do, what they are getting for their money or why there could be such a difference in price from one sofa to another.

A key question to ask yourself is what your expectations are from your furniture. Do you expect it to last twenty years? If so, then think about what you paid for your last car and how long you expected it to last. We use and abuse our furniture yet we think it should be inexpensive. It can be inexpensive, but it probably won't last. Invest in high-end materials and workmanship rather than simply in square footage.

A common mistake many people make is to buy an inexpensive sofa for the family room where they expect it to be most used. But then they purchase an expensive sofa for the formal living room where hardly anyone goes to sit. If you analyze the individual rooms in your home and make choices regarding quality based on how a piece of furniture will be used, you will go a long way toward making more of your budget.

SIMPLICITY MADE SIMPLE

To give windows a soft look without blocking light, **CHOOSE TRANSLUCENT CURTAINS**. If you have arched windows, try installing the fabric on a flexible clear rod and mount it following the shape of the arch. I tied mine back using string, then made large soft knots to create a cascading tied-back effect. It's romantic without being over the top.

A KITCHEN can be a warm and comfortable gathering place for all to enjoy. Just be sure to provide comfortable areas for guests to congregate. In my kitchen, I added a pretty carved French country bench that gives extra seating as it creates a cozy nook.

DON'T overclutter your rooms. Leave some undone spaces; it will create a feeling of clean openness.

Today's decorating style is **ALL ABOUT DETAILS**. Even the more contemporary or modern rooms have a soft touch, such as a silk throw with long streaming fringe. As with clothing styles, we are allowing ourselves the freedom to be expressive in the little touches. That translates to finding little treasures such as a single fabulous tassel to hang on a cabinet doorknob or as a tieback on your window.

If you want a **CALM ROOM** that incorporates pattern, consider using a conservative pattern on larger pieces such as a chaise or sofa. Many larger pieces of furniture can look too busy in big bold patterns. Save the bigger, bolder fabrics for smaller items such as pillows.

WORKING with florals and stripes gives you greater flexibility in designing with color, scale, and pattern because the variety of color within the pattern gives you plenty of choices to play with.

LIGHTING can be like art in a room. Consider adding decorative wall sconces to bring beauty and light to a space. They are available in a variety of prices, sizes, and finishes.

Lord, as I work to make my home
a beautiful place, please give me eyes
that see what is good in Your eyes. Help me
to give all that I have to whatever pleases You.

More on Color—
Making Choices

Nature is the most brilliant designer of all,

and the secret is in her seasons.

Each season presents a distinct array of colors,

and *your* coloring is in harmony

with one of these palettes.

—CAROLE JACKSON, *COLOR ME BEAUTIFUL*

I wrote previously about color, but there is so much more to say. The study of chromo or color therapy has been around for centuries, with an abundance of scientific data to back it up. It is important because studies show that color affects our bodies and creates biological reactions. This is why I understood when my client Kathy cried over finding just the right shade of yellow. I told her it *was* worth caring about.

You may remember from your high school science textbook that the sun emits the full spectrum of electromagnetic radiation in the form of visible white light. It travels in different wavelengths and each is perceived as a different color to the human eye. There is a different vibration level for each color, which is why even someone who is blind is sometimes able to identify colors.

This has led many scientists to believe in the benefit of color therapy because, although we are not aware of it, we are constantly absorbing these vibrations through our skin and optic nerves. Did you know medical teams are actually using color therapy to fight cancer and chronic migraines? Even athletes may benefit from light. In experimental studies, athletes gained short bursts of energy and muscle strength when exposed to red. For longer endurance, blue was used instead of red.

> We are constantly absorbing color vibrations through our skin and optic nerves.

We know that lavender walls can lull you to sleep, while green refreshes and encourages emotional growth. Orange increases confidence and can even stimulate conversation. Consequently, it's worth considering color when you want to improve the quality of your life.

Improvement starts simply with making good choices for the things you will not change often or cannot change easily. As you begin to choose the permanent finish and surface materials for your home, be sure that the colors are ones that will bring you satisfaction for the long term. Flooring, countertops, and fixtures are not easily changed; keep in mind that these products will be a part of your color scheme for a long time.

FIXTURES AND COUNTERTOPS

Remember all the pink tubs and sinks from the 1950s? Or how about the harvest gold and avocado green tubs and sinks of the seventies? And worse yet—the black tubs and toilets from the eighties! These were the worst because you could never keep them looking clean. They spotted the minute you even thought about using them. It is for this reason that I still recommend going neutral with those items, particularly bathroom fixtures and kitchen appliances.

Color is wonderful, but use it where you can change it rather easily if and when you are ready. Kitchen countertops have been gaining color over the past few years. There are so many different product options for kitchen counters that it can be very confusing.

Laminate is still the least expensive material for a countertop, but I am not seeing much of it being used because of the availability of many newer and more durable options. The most popular product seems to be granite, and other natural stones, with solid surface materials following in popularity. Natural stone obviously comes in natural colors, but it too can vary greatly. Some stones are light and neutral while others can be nearly black. If you are considering a natural stone, I highly recommend that you go directly to the stonecutter's yard and pick out a slab for yourself. It is amazing how vastly different one slab can look from another, even when they are coming from the same quarry.

Be sure you have a copy of your kitchen layout showing exactly each area where you will be using stone. Cutting stone is an art that requires the ability to use as much of the slab as possible. So every square foot is critical if you expect to get your countertop cut from the same piece. Be sure to take along a cabinet door or at least a sample of your kitchen cabinets to match colors.

Composition materials are also gaining a foothold in choices for countertops. I love the new Zodiac product that is, as I mentioned earlier, a combination of quartz and resins. It has the brilliance of real stone and the easy maintenance of a solid surface. It is available in some bold, beautiful colors such as red, purple, and yellow as well as natural shades. It is more durable than real stone, and you can be far more creative with it because it is easily cut and sculpted to any shape you desire. Like many of the other engineered stone products, Zodiac won't scratch or stain like real stone.

Wood and concrete are being touted by some for countertops, but I am not yet sold on the idea. First of all, the building industry is facing a concrete shortage, so wasting it on countertops just doesn't make sense to me, especially when there are so many other options available. Wood burns easily, needs oiling, absorbs food odor, and can blacken if water is left standing on it. Metal is another new product being used to make countertops. It is heat proof and impervious to acids and oils. However, it scratches easily and can leave a room feeling cold.

FLOORING AND CARPETS

Flooring is an area where I see the most diversity in color choices. Many people are still sticking with neutral colors, but others have started moving toward a lot of color, as we saw in the seventies. One of my clients, who works in the carpet business, chose a different color and texture of carpeting for every room in the house. It works because all of her choices are consistent with her color scheme.

Her living room has beautiful green ground carpeting with flowers in rose and cream. This room sets the tone for the rest of the first floor. It is the perfect complement to her country-cottage-style decorating. For her family room, she chose a textured sisal carpet in a medium natural tone. Her green leather sofas are accentuated with a wall unit and occasional tables that are both in rich cherry tones. Yet upstairs, in her two sons' rooms, she gave herself permission to move from the pretty cottage style and soft colors to bolder colors that make sense for boys. Both of their rooms are carpeted in plush, almost shag carpet—one in nearly navy, the other in red.

Personally, I still prefer to keep the tone of the carpet similar throughout the house and just change textures to create variety. When it comes to other types of flooring besides carpeting, hardwood floors are winning the race. They are a tried and true product that everyone appreciates. Today's wood floors are easy to care for and come in many different varieties: Many of them are prefinished, which eliminates the mess and the potential unevenness of color.

Stain colors vary from natural to medium brown tones, to deep red-toned colors. I am also seeing a lot of exotic wood flooring. One interesting wood from Africa is called Purple Heart; it is actually a purple wood. Currently, mahogany is a banned wood. Instead we are using cherry, alder, and other similar species stained to look like mahogany.

Laminate flooring is breaking ground. When it was first introduced, I wasn't too sure about it. But after nearly ten years (and lots of the kinks worked out) it is a viable, durable, easy-to-install, and very easy-to-live-with product that makes sense for today's lifestyle. Finish choices run the gamut from natural wood to faux stone to pure color.

Regardless of your choice of product, the key to a home having a simple cohesive feeling is using color to pull it all together.

SIMPLICITY MADE SIMPLE

Your **COLOR PALETTE** should have three colors: a main, a contrasting, and an accent. Use the accent color in three different places within the room to give it balance. You may add as many other colors as you wish, but remember to keep the focus on the three most important colors.

If you like patterning, the number three still applies. Be sure to choose **THREE PATTERNS** with three different scales: for example, a large floral, a medium plaid, and a small print.

TO MAINTAIN A BALANCE, use two-thirds main fabric, one-third secondary fabric, and accent with the third fabric. Make sure all patterns have the same neutral as a background. In other words, don't mix a cream background pattern with a pure white background pattern.

CHOOSE YOUR FINISH MATERIALS before finalizing your paint and fabric choices. For example, you may start out by wanting a green/beige/cream stone for your kitchen counters only to find you have fallen in love with a green/cream/black stone instead. That could make a big difference in the rest of your choices.

Always ask your plumbing and appliances suppliers to order actual **SAMPLE CHIPS** for you and keep them in your file for reference. Also, just like with paint samples, what may appear to be a neutral cream tone on the small sample can end up being peachy in reality. So be sure to check out the actual products at a showroom where they display the model.

> Lord, Your purposeful use of color amazes me.
> You refresh us with green pastures, warm us
> with orange sunsets, lift our hope with
> yellow sunflowers, strengthen us with blue skies,
> and fill our days with millions of stimulating colors
> to remind us that Your beauty is endless
> and Your power simply unquenchable.

Don't be afraid to mix and match patterns. It can add interest to a room's décor.

The key to displaying collections is to choose a constant element, whether that is color, size, or shape.

Small touches can go a long way toward making houseguests feel welcome.

A cozy bathroom with an oversized tub can be a place of
sanctuary at the end of a harried day.

Baskets provide a great tool for helping to keep kids organized.

Make use of your space in a way that meets your needs, rather than
limiting yourself to traditional uses.

Natural light is a great mood lifter, especially in a living area.

Be creative in your storage solutions. Hidden in plain sight, these towels act as an accessory.

It's important to provide workspace lighting in a kitchen, as shown here over the island and countertops.

Here, outdoor lighting and landscaping make a welcoming entryway for your guests.

Controlling Collections

"The Lord . . . has filled him with the Spirit of God,

with skill, ability and knowledge

in all kinds of crafts—to make artistic designs. . . ."

—EXODUS 35:30–32 (NIV)

Merriam-Webster's Dictionary defines clutter, in verb form, as "to fill or cover with scattered or disordered things that impede movement or reduce effectiveness." On the other hand, a collectible, as defined by Webster's, is "an object that is collected by fanciers." In my opinion, the difference between the two is what you do with them.

Early in my career as an interior designer, after working as a designer's assistant, I was hired as a senior designer in New Jersey. I was very excited about the new job and anxious to get working. My first day on the job, my boss asked me to *tchotchke* the china cabinet. Instantly, I froze—I had no idea what he meant. I was afraid I had missed some serious training in design school. Worse yet, I was afraid to ask him what he meant for fear of appearing ignorant or unworthy of the job.

Finally, I found the nerve to ask a co-worker. She laughed as she explained that it was a Yiddish term for accessorize. I laughed too as I turned beet red with embarrassment. And yet it was then that I began to understand the difference between clutter and accessories, which can completely change the personality of a room the same way jewelry can change the look of a little black dress from casual to elegant.

ACCESSORIES CAN BE PRACTICAL TOO

In the book *Clutter Control*, author Jeff Campbell says that items displayed in the house have to pass a test. Every item displayed must have a valid function or form. The author uses the example of a decorative clock that no longer keeps time but still is beautiful to look at. He suggests walking through your home and quickly testing each item displayed. Ask questions such as, Why am I keeping this? What is it doing there? Does it have a function? Does it work? Am I sick of it?

Just because you loved something ten years ago is not enough reason to keep it today unless you are still enjoying it. Just yesterday, I finally accepted the fact that the bouquet of mini-roses that a dear friend sent to me no longer looked good. I had dried and displayed them in a crystal vase on my nightstand. But the years had taken their toll—sadly, they had to go. To preserve the memory, I replaced them with a bouquet of silk roses.

Sometimes we accidentally end up with a collection. One client of mine is a pig farmer. Somewhere along the way, her family and friends decided it would be cute to buy her little ceramic pigs as gifts. Before she knew it, her house looked like a store of pigs. She may have chosen one or two of them for their artistic quality, but

> Just because you loved something ten years ago is not enough reason to keep it today.

the reality of several dozen pigs in a variety of colors, styles, and qualities was not exactly her idea of a worthy collection. As we began the restoration of her mid-1700s farmhouse, she asked me what she should do with them. She did not want to offend all her friends who had graciously gifted the little piggies to her. I suggested she photograph them and then either pack them away or give them away. If and when friends should ask about them, be honest and say it was time for a change. Then thank them for the happy memory and tell them how you thoughtfully photographed each one.

ART IS A MATTER OF DESIGN

So what is it that makes a group of things a collection? It's how you arrange them. For example, one woman hung her collection of antique handkerchiefs around the wall at the ceiling line creating a unique but amazing border. One of the simplest ways to make the most of your collection of treasures is to display them together as a unit.

My client Edward collected teapots from every place he visited. They were sporadically placed throughout the house. I suggested he gather them together and arrange them on the top of his kitchen cabinets. He was thrilled with the way they came together to make a beautiful statement that could not be made with a single teapot sitting alone.

> What makes a group of things a collection is how you arrange them.

Displaying collections is all about composition. Edward chose to use identical items. You can also choose to use an arrangement of various items. Start by examining the space you want to fill with your collectibles. Consider the vertical and the horizontal space as you begin placing items into it. If you have a wall to one side, then this will be the side you place the tallest item on. Begin working the pieces in declining heights. Or you may choose to create an artistic display by alternating heights. Stacking and varying the placement of objects from front to back will also keep it creative and add dimension. I find that the most interesting displays often contain an uneven number of items. An often-quoted phrase says that most things in nature appear in uneven numbers—God's design idea.

> The most interesting displays often contain an uneven number of items.

The biggest mistake most people make is using elements that are too small and/or are all the same size, particularly in big open spaces. If your collection is similar in size or petite, you may want to consider adding other elements to complement it. Perhaps a selection of books with some placed on their sides, others standing upright, or better yet, place a few pieces from your collection on books to vary the height. Crystal complements almost everything; a crystal vase or statue adds sparkle without detracting from the color of your treasured collection. When using a variety of items, I like to add at least one organic item to the composition for balance. An organic item is something that is from nature, for example, a plant or flowers, a rock, or even a piece of wood.

SIMPLICITY MADE SIMPLE

ALWAYS START WITH THE LARGEST or tallest item and then add items in declining height. Be sure to choose a specific item as the focal point and never confuse the eye by trying to draw attention to two items in the same arrangement. For example, if you have three items for an arrangement and two of them are nearly the same size, the eye will struggle to determine which one is more important.

SYMMETRICAL balance will always feel more formal. Asymmetrically arranged items will feel less formal. A simple way to create a balanced arrangement is to follow the lines of a triangle. The diagonal lines create an illusion that the eye perceives as more space. This is especially helpful for small areas.

Be sure to **BALANCE** your vertical elements with your horizontal elements.

Don't know where to start? Start by digging out and gathering all your treasured items. Then **ARRANGE THEM BY SIMILARITY AND SIZE.** This will get you started on what works together as a possible collection. One client had no idea how many blue and white porcelain items she owned until she went through this process. We ended up being able to dress her living room beautifully with them. They were the perfect companions for her true eighteenth-century Colonial-style room.

When working with clients, I **START BY REMOVING** all accessories from the room. Then I analyze all the surfaces to decide what is the most prominent spot to display the most important items. Don't be afraid to move things around. I do. In fact, all designers take their time with this process. No one can simply walk into a room and immediately know what to do. Instead, the process evolves one item at a time.

When working with **LARGE-SCALE ITEMS**, be sure to allow breathing room so each item can be seen. You can leave as much as twelve inches around each item in a large area.

TO SAFELY DISPLAY a collection, consider a shadow box or display table that keeps your valuables clean and safe. There are many styles available to easily match your room.

One way to bring together a great look without creating the look of clutter is to use items that are **ALL THE SAME COLOR**. For example, one of my clients loves contemporary glass vases. I suggested she stick to purchasing just one color. She may choose any shape and size she likes. Keeping the color consistent unites them to create a single artistic statement.

> Lord, help me to artfully exhibit the treasures
> that have been added to my life. And give me
> the wisdom to know when it's time to lay
> aside burdens that only clutter my life.

Environment Affects
Intimate Relationships

A cheerful look brings joy to the heart,

and good news gives health to the bones.

—PROVERBS 15:30 (NIV)

We feel better when we hear good news, and we feel better when someone simply smiles at us. A kind word, gentle smile, or simple gesture brings us joy. Interior designer Rysia Suchecka writes, "It is the cumulative impact of little things that profoundly affects our sensory enrichment." I believe you will be better if you feel better. After all, how can you be miserable when you see a magnificent sky? I know I can't. Yet we have the opportunity for such beauty every day and don't often take advantage of it.

The same is true for our homes. I recently did a radio interview where we discussed how important the master bedroom is to women. It doesn't seem to matter as much to the guys. But when a woman has a beautiful bedroom that speaks to her heart, all of life is better. Just ask the guys who finally let their wives decorate the bedroom about the difference it has made in their lives!

CREATE A NESTING NOOK

When I was single, my bedroom was my nest—my sanctuary. I could live in my bedroom. Actually, I practically did. When I came home in the evenings it was usually dark. My cats and I would settle in for the night in the king-size bed with the down comforter. It was perfectly peaceful. When Dave and I married, things obviously changed. The bedroom took on a whole new dimension, as it should. But for me, as a woman, it still had to be pretty.

Too many women assume that their husbands won't sleep in a pretty room. The reality is that men will sleep anywhere that is comfortable! One of the sweetest things that happened when Dave and I married is that he automatically started making the bed each morning. This simple gesture touched my heart. I appreciate the care he takes each morning in making our bed, and I was surprised at how affected I was by this small act of gentleness. Whenever I tell this to couples, I often hear that the husband also began making the bed soon after hearing our story. I think it's because the husbands saw how touched I was by this gesture and they wanted to give this thoughtful gift to their wives as well.

Merriam-Webster's Dictionary defines the bedroom as "a room furnished with a bed and intended primarily for sleeping." Most of us no longer have the luxury of using any room in our home for only one purpose. Our bedrooms have also become our home offices, exercise gyms, and dens. The key is to find creative ways of using space to accommodate our lives while still creating an intimate and beautiful couple's retreat. As the most personal space within the home, the bedroom should be a place where we retreat for solitude, to think, ponder, and

> Too many women assume that their husbands won't sleep in a pretty room.

process. It can also be a "nesting" place filled with books, pets, your favorite music, and more. And shouldn't it also be romantic?

Recently while working on the master bedroom with a young couple, we discussed their vision for the room. As I prompted Connie and Adam to close their eyes and imagine the possibilities—they both responded with one word: "romantic." But when they opened their eyes they saw a treadmill, a collection of assorted odds and ends, a laundry basket, makeshift draperies, and a bed that was too large for the space. Most importantly

> The reality is that men will sleep anywhere that is comfortable!

though, it was devoid of color, except for a quilt that, although beautiful, was not romantic. I must tell you they had just returned from a weekend couple's retreat. Obviously, it was the perfect time to be discussing renovations to the bedroom.

ACCESSORIZE WITH THINGS YOU LOVE

Connie had made the quilt that was on the bed. As she explained, it was the first and would be the last quilt she would ever make. It had taken her over a year to finish. It was bright blue, white, red, and yellow. It was far from romantic. But because Connie had worked so hard on this quilt she was determined to use it whether she liked it or not. It was funny watching her blood pressure rise as she told us what a pain this quilt had been to make. Clearly this was not a joyful memory. Nonetheless, it was on the bed.

I tried to diplomatically discuss the possibility of removing it from the bedroom and was not very successful. Finally, her husband got down on his knee, took her hand in his and pleaded. It was quite a sight. It wasn't long before we were all laughing. With further coaxing, Adam and I convinced Connie that it would be okay to pack the quilt and will it to some grandchild of the future. That opened the way for us to create a space that met both their needs.

Red was the color they both felt was romantic. Their dream-home style would be a restored farmhouse with old and new country-style furnishings. And although they live in a newly constructed home, there was no reason we couldn't have an upscale country look for their bedroom. After eliminating the laundry accouterments, and repositioning the treadmill in a corner of the closet, we found a soft red and cream toile wallpaper to set the mood. We complemented it with a silk plaid of reds and creams for the draperies and pillows. A new quilted cream-colored comforter and an abundance of beautifully detailed pillows finished the bed. Soft, plush carpeting completed the look.

For many families, the master bedroom is often the place where children want to come when they have something important to talk about. My friend Jan's children come in for "flop and chat" on a regular basis. As teenagers, flopping on the bed is the most natural thing to do. Jan knows when an otherwise nonchatty son flops on the bed, it's important. Her children also know, however, that if the door is shut, it means it is mom and dad's time alone.

SIMPLICITY MADE SIMPLE

Of all the rooms in the house, **YOUR BEDROOM**, and in particular the color of its walls, requires special care because it sets the stage for your dreams at night and is the first impression you will have when you wake up.

VERSATILITY is key to making your bedroom do double duty. For example, a small table can be used as a desk and a nightstand. Use the vertical space. I built a floor-to-ceiling bookcase with a depth of sixteen inches that provides great storage while keeping the room from looking cluttered. I painted it white to match the woodwork so it feels like a part of the room without becoming the focal point.

San Francisco interior designer Michael Tedrick says, "It's a myth that men don't like 'pretty' bedrooms. Men take to beautiful bedrooms with fine linens the way they take to Lacoste shirts and well-worn jeans." A few smart moves can give your bedroom an updated look. Start by restyling your bed. **TRY A FITTED SLIPCOVER** to change the appearance of your bed. Even a wood headboard can be covered. If you like, you can add a little foam padding first—simply tape it in place. Then cover it with a fabric of your choice.

For a recent **BEDROOM MAKEOVER**, I made an upholstered headboard and mounted it directly to the wall. I had plywood cut to shape. Then with a spray adhesive, I padded the board with foam, adding extra padding around the edges. Then I stapled a new headboard with a prequilted white cotton duck fabric. The client was thrilled!

TO CREATE A TIMELESS LOOK, never let the current trends dictate your style. Instead, select vintage and new furniture for your room. The best design is usually an evolving process. I love to work with opposing styles such as an ornately carved bed and simple style chest or armoire. I also believe less is more, particularly in a bedroom. I believe a less cluttered look is peaceful and more conducive to becoming calm. Clutter—well, it does just that—clutters the mind as well as the room.

ACCESSORIES are a great way to add color and personality to a room without spending a fortune. Choose only things you love—things that will bring long-lasting pleasure. Two of my favorite accessories were found at a flea market. One is a beautiful canvas painting of flowers. The other is a crackled old serving tray in sea foam green. Both are displayed on the bookcase in the bedroom.

NEVER FORGET FLOWERS; they are one of God's most beautiful works of art. A cluster of roses in a simple vase says more than words ever could. Today's style of arranging flowers is natural. Cut your stems so the bloom is just above the top of the vase. You may want to arrange the flowers in your hand first and then place them into the vase.

Lord, thank You for granting sleep to those You love. You said that in vain one rises early, and stays up late toiling for food (Psalm 127:2). Thank You for reminding me that You are watching over us as we obediently rest in Your grace.

Appealing to the Senses

I will be unafraid. Especially, I will not be afraid
to be happy, to enjoy what is beautiful, to love,
and to believe that those I love, love me.

—AUTHOR UNKNOWN

When you think about being happy, what do you think about? Are you afraid of happiness? Years ago, I had a friend who wasn't happy unless she was miserable. It took me a couple of years to realize this. She was always in crisis. No matter how well her life was going, she always found something seriously wrong with it. Eventually, she wore me out. I simply could not continue to live in her perpetual crisis mode. She was always waiting for happiness; she lived for the "if only's" to make her happy. *If only* she could find a good husband, she would be happy. *If only* she had another degree of education, she would be happy. She found a husband, got yet another degree, and still was not happy. The problem was that she never enjoyed what she had.

As you began reading this book, what did you expect *simplicity* to do for you? Steve Stephens, psychologist and author of *Lists to Live By For Simplicity*, says that simplicity should ease our stress, clear away clutter, increase our appreciation, clarify our priorities, purify our hearts, uplift our spirits, settle our emotions, encourage our friends, deepen our peace, and build our character. Does that sound like happiness to you?

Interior designer Rysia Suchecka says, "Design should not only provoke sight, but also touch, hearing, sound, and smell, and it should possess tactile qualities. When we bring a new focus to the small components of life, like setting a table for every meal and lighting candles . . . we change our lives for the better."

I agree with her. I believe it is the simple things that we can add to our daily living that will most enhance our lives by making us consciously aware of all the beauty and joy life has to offer.

> Simple things can enhance our lives by making us aware of all the beauty and joy life has to offer.

Everything about a house—the room layout, furniture, lighting, colors, acoustics, and even where art is hung on the walls—can support certain feelings and behavior patterns. As Rysia says, I believe that by meeting our sensory needs, we can improve the quality of our lives. What are some small changes or additions that you could bring to your home that would help improve your quality of life within it?

As I work with clients, I pay particular attention to which senses are their strongest. Many of us are tactile, which means the fabrics we choose must feel soft and comfortable to the touch. Just as the commercial for cotton fiber says, "it is the fabric of our lives"—because it *feels* good.

THE SCENT AND SOUND OF HOME

Within our homes, there are other senses, such as smelling and hearing, that we can please. Most of us are already aware of the powerful emotional effects that scent can have on us. Perhaps you have read about how the scent of pumpkin pie can improve the love life between a wife and her husband. And there is a plethora of books on essential oils and the specific ways to use them. I grow lavender in my garden because it is one of my favorite scents. It calms me to sleep at night and it soothes my aching muscles when added to bath oil for soaking. I also grow catnip for our cats. It's remarkable the responses we get from Percy and Peony with this simple plant.

Sound has also proven to be a powerful way to enhance or detract from the quality of your home. When working in someone's home, I often perform a *scream test*. If it is a two-story home, I start by standing on the stairs and screaming. I do this so I can hear how far sound travels. I repeat this process throughout the house to determine how best to create a home that is quiet when you want it to be. I also flush toilets and listen to where the sound travels. I have spent too many gracious meals in dining rooms that happened to be next to the wall of the toilet flush pipe. It astounds me that builders don't think about this when they are planning the plumbing.

> Pleasing scents and sounds can enhance our psychological and physical well-being.

Scientists have known for centuries that welcome sounds such as classical or folk music will have a positive effect and enhance our psychological and physical well-being. The opposite is also true: unpleasant sounds can irritate and even anger us. Controlling sound within your home is a simple but important way to bring more happiness to your family. Something as basic as moving the entertainment center to the opposite wall from bedrooms can make a huge difference in how sound travels within your home.

I am always astonished when I dine at a nice restaurant to find I cannot even hear myself think because no one thought about the acoustics as part of the design plan. My brother says I have sonar ears. He swears I can hear ten miles away. Perhaps I do have sensitive hearing, nonetheless I believe we all need a little silence in our lives. As a result, I attempt to add some sound-absorbing materials to every room to help make life quieter. This is especially important for busy families with children.

I come from a family of six children. At one time five of us were taking music lessons. Unfortunately for my parents, we each played a different instrument. At practice time, we started with a violin player in the basement, an accordion player (me) in the family room, a coronet in the dining room, my brother with guitar in his bedroom, and the finale, my sister playing drums in the garage. The cacophony of noise throughout our house at practice hour was more than nerve-wracking. God bless my parents. They were amazing to be able to live through that. And a few blessings for our neighbors in the summer too, because we did not have air-conditioning, which means the entire neighborhood was treated to our impromptu concerts through our open windows.

No matter what the needs are for you in your home, you can always find something that will make it more peaceful and pleasing to the senses.

SIMPLICITY MADE SIMPLE

Since many of today's homes are using hard-flooring products, rather than wall-to-wall carpeting, the use of **THICK AREA RUGS** and carpets can help prevent sound from moving between floors. Be sure to add a pad beneath the carpets to add further sound absorption.

By simply **PLACING AN AREA RUG** under the main furniture within a room, you can keep things quieter.

WINDOWS are one of the foremost ways for outside noises to get in. Be sure to recaulk around doors and windows when needed. In addition, since glass is a conductor of noise, it may be necessary to replace single-pane windows with double- or triple-paned glass instead.

If you are planning a renovation in your home that includes changing floor products, **CONSIDER A FLOATING FLOOR PRODUCT.** Floating floors are laid over an existing floor, often with a layer of material between them, trapping noise between the two layers. This is a great way to add a lot of sound absorption to a room.

If your family is like ours was, and the music's beat is sending a strong impulse of pain directly to your head, try **BUILDING A PORTABLE SOUND BARRIER** with panels to surround your talented musicians.

Did you ever notice how a voice travels through the air ducts? It is amazing. Did you know you could actually paint your ductwork with liquid soundproofing? You can. You can also choose to **COVER THE AIR DUCTS** with soundproof matting.

One way to **SOUNDPROOF ROOMS** is to apply sound-absorbing material directly on the doors. For example, if your teenagers like to live loudly in the finished basement, consider padding the basement side of the door. It won't stop all the noise, but it will deaden it. You can also purchase new and improved interior doors that have insulation inside. The old hollow doors did nothing to help with noise, but these new doors are great.

DON'T FORGET your walls—they too can be an easy way to quiet things down. A simple solution is to hang sound-absorbing, fabric-wrapped wall panels, available in specialty stores or online. They are usually contemporary in style and are great for recreation rooms and game rooms. They have been used in offices for years. If all else fails, buy a pair of sound-blocking headsets; that way you can choose just what you want to hear!

Father, Your Word says that we can do nothing
better than to eat and drink and find satisfaction
in our work. But without You, who can eat or find
enjoyment? Help me to be fully aware, with all
of my senses, of Your presence in my daily life.
Teach me to enjoy the simple pleasures that
are freely given to those who please You.

PART FOUR

Maintaining a Simple Home

PERHAPS THE MOST DIFFICULT STEP to achieving a simple home is maintaining it through the everyday use. Being organized, even in the unseen corners of your home, will help you enjoy stepping into your house at the end of a hectic day. We're going to dig deep and learn to throw away what is no longer needed and preserve what is precious so that you can thrive in a home that is both pleasing and practical.

Lead and Delegate

According to all that the Lord commanded Moses,
so the children of Israel made all the work.
And Moses did look upon all the work, and, behold,
they had done it as the Lord had commanded,
even so had they done it: and Moses blessed them.

—EXODUS 39:42–43 (KJV)

There is a lot to consider when it comes to managing a household. Just as Moses had to learn skills to lead and manage the Israelites, so shall we if we are to manage our homes successfully. Great leaders like Moses gave important responsibilities to others, like his brother Aaron, and then trusted them to do the job. Moses planned and directed while letting others participate on the team. If you are the leader of your home, then you need to determine who can best be trusted to get each specific job done.

Unfortunately, even in the best of circumstances, it seems a few people do most of the work. It's because once we learn who are the most dependable, it simply makes sense to give them the work to be done. We know we can count on them. As the old phrase goes, "If you want something done, give it to a busy person." The problem is that eventually, the responsible/busy person can feel overwhelmed and taken advantage of.

In reality, we don't mean to take advantage of others. We appreciate the work of others, but with busy lives it's easy to miss opportunities to express gratitude. Often this problem can be compounded by the fact that if someone who does not ordinarily step up to the task does do something to help, we go overboard to thank them for it; this can make the more reliable person feel even more slighted.

SIMPLY GIVE THANKS

My friend Jan is the best at remembering to thank everyone. Even with a blended family of eight children, she manages to send thank-you notes. She is amazing, which just proves that with some effort, we can all do a better job of thanking those who help us manage every day.

Too often, the delegation of tasks is not planned. Instead, it just happens. The best way to ease the management of a household is to determine who is good at what. Sometimes our strengths can become weaknesses. Jan and I have often discussed how we are similar in our strengths to take charge, pay attention to detail, and basically get the job done.

The problem is that we sometimes find it easier to just do it ourselves, rather than delegate to someone who may or may not do as good a job as we can do ourselves. This means, before we know it, we are the ones in charge of everything. That's okay, if we really want to be in charge of everything, and are in a position to find the time to get it done without being stressed by it. Unfortunately, that is rarely the case. This is an excellent example of strength becoming a weakness. Instead, we should be training others to do more.

Habit also plays a big part in who does what. Just because you have always been the one to handle a particular job doesn't mean you have to continue doing it. It may just be a bad habit. It is worth reevaluating our areas of giftedness and using them as the criteria for delegating tasks.

It's wonderful when I meet couples who have taken the time to look at each other's areas of skill and giftedness and make the division of tasks work. Both of my brothers are excellent cooks. In addition, they have a loving, nurturing way with children. When my married brother's children were young, they would hang on daddy's legs instead of mom's when they were upset. It was only natural for their situation.

> Stress can be self-induced. Examine your habits and take charge of de-stressing your life.

Both of my brothers are the perfect candidates for being in charge of cooking, grocery shopping, and caring for the children. In a two-income family, that means their wives (let's hope) enjoy doing lawn work and cleaning the house and paying bills. My married brother has just that arrangement. And it has worked perfectly for many years. His wife is the driver whenever they take a long trip, which makes sense because she is a professional bus driver. This is her area of skill.

Sometimes we have to think outside the box to manage our households most effectively. My friend Deb also comes from a two-income family. She believes that it is important for the family to sit down together for dinner. When Deb evaluated the situation, she realized that she would rather clean house with her limited time than cook meals. Her solution, although unusual, makes perfect sense: She located a local gal whose entrepreneurial business is to cook for busy families. Deb simply provided the cook with the family's food preferences, and with plastic food storage containers. Each meal is labeled and can be frozen until the family is ready to heat and eat. It's the perfect solution! Budgetwise, it costs very little more than if Deb shopped and cooked herself. The time she saves, in addition to the quality family time gained, makes this a very good investment.

I had a similar cooking dilemma while in college. I was working full-time and going to school. (This was the premicrowave era.) My friend Krissy was a stay-at-home single mom with three children. We decided to share cooking. She cooked during the week and I cooked on the weekends. She got weekends off from cooking and I got a home-cooked meal every night during the week, a simple strategy that made both our lives better. (FYI—Krissy still makes the best cornbread muffins!)

> Sometimes we have to think outside the box to manage our households most effectively.

Ultimately, managing a household is a matter of determining just what *needs* to get done, what can be eliminated, and how best to handle the priorities. We have to pay our bills, we have to eat, and it would be nice to have a clean home. I would also like some leisure time, which means I have to carve out time from my existing schedule to make time for what I want to do.

Home magazine did a survey, which was published in its July/August 2004 issue, regarding the hidden habits of American homeowners. It asked what spending time with your family at home means. The unfortunate answers below are a sad commentary on society's overextended schedules:

5%	Eating in shifts
11%	Doing homework with the kids
17%	Getting on each other's nerves
67%	Watching TV together

It's apparent that if we are going to improve the quality of our lives, we must make changes in how and what we are doing. I hope your family statistics fare better than do those above.

SIMPLICITY MADE SIMPLE

MAINTAIN A FAMILY CALENDAR in a central location that all members can easily use. Be sure that each member of the family knows he or she is responsible for writing in upcoming events. If anyone discovers a conflict, a discussion with the family must be arranged to decide how to handle it. A simple way to keep the schedule clear is to assign a different color pen or marker to each family member.

My mom always kept a **CHORE SCHEDULE** hung on the wall. It was the best way to keep us kids from using the excuse "I forgot!" Most children are capable of simple tasks like table setting, table clearing, cooking (yes, cooking—that's how all six of us kids got to be good cooks), doing dishes, grocery shopping (Mom or Dad should prepare the grocery list), yard work, trash collection, bathroom cleaning, and, of course, cleaning their own rooms!

WORKING AS A TEAM is a great way to get things done. Consider pairing up children to take on home chores together. Make it fun; play tag team against the clock.

Create good habits by getting everyone in the family into the routine of preparing as much as possible **THE NIGHT BEFORE**. For example, it is easy to choose clothes, arrange your briefcase or book bag, pack lunches, and locate keys, purse, and so on before bed.

A simple way to keep clutter to a minimum is to be sure that everyone takes fifteen minutes each day to **PICK UP AROUND THE HOUSE**. Just think how much cleaner your home would be if all of you agreed to pick up ten items a day and put them away.

HIRE HELP. Neither my husband nor I have the time or the desire to deal with our large yard. We decided, in the interest of all, it was best to hire a service to handle this aspect of our lives. It has eliminated nagging and guilt over who does the yard work, or when it should be done. Perhaps you can do as my friend Maria has done: Recruit a neighbor to mow your lawn for ten dollars a week.

I keep a running **SHOPPING (NONGROCERY) LIST**. This makes it easy for everyone in the family to add what is needed to the list. Even children can add items such as shampoo, school supplies, whatever. If it's not on the list, they have the option of purchasing it themselves or going without. It won't take long for them to learn to be responsible if they know they won't have what they need unless they write it on the list.

Be sure to **PLAN FOR SELF-CARE**. I schedule a massage once a month. If I didn't plan for one hour a month just for me, it would never happen. The same can be true for exercise. A healthy body is good for the mind and is needed for managing a functional home.

> Father, thank You for giving talent to those
> around me. Help me to recognize the strengths
> of others, share the work and reward them
> for doing a good job. I realize that taking time
> to work together builds unity and good memories.
> Bless us when we use our strengths to strengthen others.

The Rhythm of Home and Life

So the Israelites did everything
the Lord commanded Moses;
that is the way they encamped
under their standards,
and that is the way they set out,
each with his own clan and family.

—NUMBERS 2:34 (NIV)

God's command for orderliness served the same purpose as order serves a sports team: safety, efficiency, and organization. Chaos ensues when a group or team disintegrates into a mob of individuals each going his or her own way. If a group unites and seeks God's wisdom and direction for organization, its effectiveness is enhanced. God's design is always perfect. If God were in charge of making your home operate more efficiently, then it would run like clockwork.

One of the basic principles of organization is thinking before you act. If you logically think through the task at hand, you will make better choices for accomplishing the work. Planning is the second key to being organized. If we don't take the time to think about what we need to accomplish and plan for the best time and way to accomplish it, we will continue to operate the way we always have—without regard to effectiveness.

Unfortunately, most of us feel as though we don't have enough time in the day to rethink or plan for change. Most of us are happy to just get through the day. Change is hard and can be a slow process, but it is worth the effort and time invested.

> The key to sorting and eliminating excess items is to do it quickly.

I am sure you have heard the old story of the young wife who sliced off the end of the ham she was preparing for dinner. Her husband had been watching and asked her why she cut the end off. She said, because her mother always did. They decided to call her mom to find out the answer. Her mom's response was the same as hers, "because my mother always did." Finally, upon calling Grandma, they got the answer: Grandma didn't have a pan large enough for the size of the ham! It's so easy to do things the same old way without ever questioning why—even when it makes absolutely no sense.

I encourage you to particularly examine the things you do every day. For example, do you struggle with pulling together your wardrobe for the day? If so, why? Is it because you have trouble locating items in your closet or dresser? That would be a sure sign that it's time to clean and simplify your wardrobe areas. There is a television show called *Clean Sweep*, where the homeowners are instructed to trash, sell, or keep items in a short period of time. This is the perfect approach to eliminating almost any source of too much stuff within a home.

The key to sorting and eliminating excess items is to do it quickly. Do not allow yourself time to ponder your decision because hesitation will almost certainly result in keeping more than you should.

Timing is everything. Too often, we put off until later things we should simply do now. Procrastination will only lead to more work—more things to put away, and more things to clean. As the apt old phrase goes, if you don't have time to do it right, when will you find time to do it over?

As an exercise, I set the timer to see how long it would take for the simple task of handling laundry. It took only five minutes for me to fold and put away a load of mixed white clothing—and that included answering one solicitation phone call. When I was growing up, our folded laundry often would sit on top of the washer and dryer for days. It drove me crazy. As a result, I have never left laundry piled on the machines unless there was an emergency.

Frederick Winslow Taylor was a time expert for Midvale Steel Works in Philadelphia in 1878. He conducted experiments to determine how to work most effectively. His most valuable tool was watching workers' hands to see if they used both of them efficiently. He would then arrange their tools to permit better sequence of motion. A motion-minded person uses both hands effectively. Research shows that a right-handed person works most effectively from left to right. This will automatically improve the rhythm of your work, which usually improves the speed at which you do things.

Something as simple as putting groceries away while returning phone calls can save you many minutes to use later in the day. Often I clean out a kitchen drawer while talking on the phone. If contemplating this idea gives you a pain in the neck, get a headset or a hands-free earpiece for your phone. My sister has one and loves it.

Ever wonder how well-organized your kitchen is? Try inviting a friend or family member to cook in your home. Or even better, hire a local chef who offers this service. I guarantee you will quickly know the good and bad news about your kitchen.

CLEAN IT AND STORE IT IN AN ASSIGNED SPACE

There are seasons and rhythms to all our work. If we take the time to clean things before we put them away, then when we need them next season they will be ready to go. This is true of seasonal clothing and seasonal items such as garden equipment and Christmas decorations. Having a specific place for every item will not only make everyday tasks easier, but will eventually lead to finding more time for yourself rather than wasting time looking for items.

> A made bed provides motivation to keep the rest of the room in order.

Do you have to think twice when someone asks where the outdoor extension cord is for the Christmas lights? Not a good sign. Those seasonal items should certainly have a home that is well-marked and simple to find.

One way to see how efficiently you have managed organization in your home is to pretend you are blind. With your eyes closed, could you accomplish getting dressed, making breakfast and filing away the day's mail? These are simple tasks that you perform every day; the items needed should be placed in areas so defined that you could locate them in the dark.

Have you subscribed to the idea that making a bed is a waste of time because you are only going to sleep in it again? That kind of thinking can really lead to trouble. Soon you will be saying, "Why clean the house? It will only get dirty again." A home needs daily attention. No matter how you try, the work will never really be done. However, if everything is returned to its proper place daily, your home will stay organized and take less time to clean.

A good way to look at your home is by dividing necessary maintenance into daily, weekly, monthly, and yearly segments. Then schedule it. I schedule time to pay bills by literally writing it into my schedule twice a month. I know that I must block out two hours for each bill-paying period. During that time I record every check I write in my money-management system. This diligence pays off big time when tax time arrives. I simply define the spending reports based on categories and print them out for the accountant.

I had a surprise arrive with the Sunday newspaper today. It was a free sample of a disposable toilet bowl cleaning brush. I love it! (Okay, I admit I am weird.) Who knew something so seemingly insignificant could be so cool? After trying it out, I realized this is an answer to a prayer—well maybe not prayer—but it does make cleaning the toilet so much more convenient. If your home is like mine, you have more than one toilet to clean. And unlike other things in the house, sometimes you can't wait until the scheduled day to clean it. Now, by simply keeping a disposable pad and handle in each bathroom, I can easily clean it when necessary without running down to the supply closet. I think this is marvelous!

The goal for planning and implementing a home-maintenance system is to find more free time for the things you enjoy doing rather than those you have to do.

SIMPLICITY MADE SIMPLE

Here is a sample seven-day schedule to help you begin your organizational planning process:

1. **A FAMILY WORKDAY**—This is the day that every person in the family can expect to contribute to the maintenance of the household, such as mowing the lawn, washing the car, and so on.

2. **DESK DAY**—Spend time paying bills at your desk, balancing your checkbook, answering letters, and planning family activities such as vacations.

3. **A FULL CLEANING DAY**—Clean a different part of your house until it is dejunked. Spend this time cleaning your closets, or scrubbing and polishing surfaces that only need this intense work every few months.

4. **A HALF-DAY OF CLEANING**—Take care of the laundry, dust, remove pet fur on the carpets (or in my case—cleaning up Miss Peony's hairballs) and toothpaste blobs in the sinks, and so forth.

5. **A GO-FER DAY**—This is the day reserved for running to the grocery store, bank, dry cleaners, hardware store, post office, or anywhere else your errands lead.

6. **A PLAY DAY FOR YOU**—Plug in some time for yourself to read, paint, or do lunch with friends. I love a day when I can plan a nap!

7. **A FAMILY DAY**—This is a day to do whatever makes the family feel rested.

Lord, thank You for making a time
for every purpose under heaven. Teach us to balance
the rhythm of work, worship, rest, and recreation.
Help us to use what You have given us
to enjoy, and also learn to put
away the things that are no longer useful.

Leave No Pile Unturned—
Get Organized

Concerning the divisions of the porters:

Of the Korhites

was Meshelemiah the son of the Kore,

of the sons of Asaph.

—1 CHRONICLES 26:1 (KJV)

Did you know that the temple that Solomon built had four thousand porters? The jobs that were assigned to them are explained in 1 Chronicles 9. Some of their duties included: checking out the equipment and utensils used each day and making sure they were returned to their proper storage area; storing, ordering, and maintaining the food supplies for the priests and sacrifices; caring for the furniture; mixing incense that was burned daily; and accounting for the gifts brought. Wouldn't you love to have even a few of those porters helping to run your house?

It's obvious that organization was mandated as an important element to maintaining a sacred space (and don't our homes qualify?) even in biblical times. Knowing this certainly justifies the need to be organized. The reality is that disorganization robs us of time and quality of life.

> I will admit that I am a pile maker. As an interior designer and an author, it would be impossible for me to file away all the fabric, carpet, flooring, and wallpaper samples. They simply don't fit into a normal file system. I am a visual person, which means "out of sight, out of mind." Therefore, it is necessary for me to keep piles around until I have finished the work. As an author, I leave the resource materials on my desk and on the floor around my desk for the following day's writing. That way when I come down to work in the morning, I can simply get going without looking for everything I need to get started. I call this organized chaos. This does not mean that yesterday's piles are still lying about; they are put away and organized. This is a system that works for me.

One of my dear friends, Stephanie Carbaugh, is a professional organizer. I love the name of her company: Sensible Resolution for Chaos. Isn't that fun? It is the perfect description for what she does. Stephanie says the first thing you need to remember is that Rome was not built in a day—neither is organization. She also says that organization doesn't have to look pretty; it needs to function for you. She suggested two questions to ask yourself:

1. Are you unable to find what you need in a short period of time, say five minutes or less?
2. Does the area that you work in—or look at—cause you stress?

Disorganization can rob us of time and quality of life.

Stephanie says that if you answered yes to either question, you need to make changes in organization, and you may need help. Her suggested follow-up question is, How much clutter do you like to function in? Some of us actually need some clutter to function well. Stephanie also says that you need to create organization systems that mesh with your personality and style. She reminds you to keep in mind your "team" at home or at work that needs to function with you.

Organization will look different at different times of your life. For example, my assistant Patty says that when her children were young, she was happy to just get the clothes washed and dried. If they didn't make it out of the laundry basket and get put away, it didn't matter. The main thing was that they were clean! We must remember to give ourselves a break during certain times of life. If you are going through big changes, relax a little on the organization. The key to a functional home is that it meets your needs. The goal is *not* to be a slave to the home or organization system.

There is a time to search and a time to give up, a time to keep and a time to throw away (Stephanie's paraphrase of Ecclesiastes 3). I love that! It helps us to face reality. After all, isn't facing reality what life is about? If you want to succeed at conquering the clutter in your life, you will need to dedicate time to planning a blueprint for success. Most professional organizers will tell you that means devoting three weeks to the hard work of examining, trying on, evaluating, storing, tossing out, and giving away stuff. The easiest way to do this is to *zone* your areas/needs for organization. Julie Morgenstern, in her book *Organizing from the Inside Out*, uses the acronym SPACE to define the process of getting organized.

> Organization will look different at different times of your life.

S – Sort
P – Purge
A – Access
C – Containerize
E – Equalize (maintain)

So many of us are overwhelmed with the idea of beginning the process of organizing. We simply don't tackle it because it's just too daunting a task to begin with. Stephanie Carbaugh reminds us of the old joke, "How do you eat an elephant? One bite at a time." The same is true with organization. Do not bite off more than you should. The key is taking small pieces at a time.

Did you ever wonder what the term *paper tiger* means? I believe the paper tiger is the mountain of paper we keep in our homes. Finding a way to eliminate or file away paper in a manner that it can easily be found is a huge challenge. I have read numerous books about organization over the years. What I discovered is that overall, I am pretty good at handling paper. My system may not be exactly what the experts recommend, but it works for me. That is the key to all systems—they must work for you. Barbara Hemphill designed a software program called *The Paper Tiger*, which is an excellent system for home and work. She says that eighty percent of the paperwork that we keep we will never use and most likely not find. She also says that forty percent of it can safely be tossed. Imagine the difference that ridding your home of forty percent of the paperwork would make.

> Take small steps when beginning the process of organizing your home. It will help you avoid feeling overwhelmed.

One helpful method of dealing with paper that has worked for me is to open my mail each day standing with the wastebasket by my side. This allows me to get rid of any junk mail, as well as all the unnecessary envelopes and miscellaneous paperwork, immediately. I then place the day's mail into a basket that I keep at the top of the stairs leading to my home office. The basket is just large enough to handle about two weeks' worth of mail. That forces me to deal with all of it every two weeks.

SIMPLICITY MADE SIMPLE

Most professional organizers will tell you that if you cannot afford to hire them, then absolutely **ENLIST THE HELP OF A FRIEND**. I suggest a buddy system where you help each other get organized. The friend plays the role of assistant. The assistant is the one who asks pertinent questions such as, "Does it require action? Is it recent enough to be beneficial? Would it be difficult to locate this information elsewhere if you ever needed it? Does it have tax or legal ramifications?" These are some simple questions, but they can make a big dent in your paperwork piles.

We all want to **DONATE** to worthy causes. But once you make a donation to one group, you suddenly can end up on what seems like every worthy cause's mailing list. My solution to dealing with this issue is to treat the donation mail the same as my bills. I include them with the two-week pay period. If I decide during that pay period not to send them money, then I throw out their solicitation. That way I don't have a pile of stuff that I never get to. Believe me, they will give you another chance to donate, and it's probably already in the mail to you.

It's a common trap to believe you'll have time to read all the magazines clamoring for your attention. **MAKE A DECISION** as to how many magazines is enough.

I must read hundreds of professional journals and magazines a year; it's part of my job. My solution is to quickly—while standing—page through and **RIP OUT THOSE ARTICLES THAT I AM MOST INTERESTED IN**. I keep those articles in a pile near my reading chair and, I must admit, in the bathroom wall-hung magazine rack. I then spend ten to fifteen minutes each day reading them. I have found the best time to read most of them is immediately after I have read the evening newspaper.

A key to organizing paper is having a place to put it. One simple idea is to **USE THREE-RING BINDERS**. Compile and file into binders by such categories as scheduled maintenance, exterior maintenance, planned improvements, insurance policies, and warranties. This is also a great way to organize your children's activities, such as sports. For example, if your son plays football, this is a good place to keep all schedules, memos and equipment requirements.

LEGAL AND TAX PAPERWORK is confusing. Since we aren't sure how long we need to keep it, we keep it forever. This is not a good plan. Here are some basic guidelines: The statute of limitation on tax returns is three years. So many will tell you that you are safe if you keep tax returns three years. However, most professionals would caution you to keep them for six years.

You should keep records that **SUPPORT YOUR TAX RETURNS** for six years. They include the following:

- ➤ 1098 (interest payments on mortgage, bank loans, credit cards)
- ➤ 1099 (miscellaneous income), 1099B (proceeds from sales of securities), 1099R (pension)
- ➤ K-1's (partnership/subchapter-S share of distribution)
- ➤ W-2/W-2P (wages, tax withholding), W-4 (withholding allowances)
- ➤ Business use of a home or auto, and business income and expense records
- ➤ Education expenses
- ➤ IRS correspondence
- ➤ Medical and dental expenses
- ➤ Charitable contribution receipts
- ➤ Records in connection with any and all property, and stock records
- ➤ Records for capital gains and losses
- ➤ Taxes (personal property, real estate, state)

Father, Your Word says that You are not the author of confusion but of peace. You do all things decently and in order. Lord, I ask for the wisdom to know how to keep my life and home in order so that peace dwells here with us.

Attics and Garages and Basements, Oh My!

And they answered Joshua, saying,

All that thou commandest us we will do,

and whithersoever thou sendest us, we will go.

—JOSHUA 1:16 (KJV)

Chaos would have ensued and God's chosen people surely would have failed if everyone had decided to conquer the Promised Land on their own. In order to accomplish the enormous task of occupying the land, everyone had to agree to the leader's plan and be willing to support and obey by going wherever he led.

If you accept me as your leader to reorganize your house, you will be agreeing to take on an enormous task of your own and you will be sent into the darkest, dampest, deepest, scariest parts of your home. You must pledge to yourself to commit to the plan and obey the rules that will be set forth for success. Are you ready?

Let's start with some basic rules that will apply for all three areas to be conquered. You must accept the fact that this is a *huge* job and it will require hard work.

You will get dirty. You will get frustrated and perhaps sentimental. Do not let any of this keep you from moving forward with the goal. It will be worth the effort.

When tackling any project of this nature it is necessary to know whether enlisting your family members will help or hinder the process. The last thing you need is a committee voting on whether to keep the old volleyball net. Be honest as you consider your family dynamics. Perhaps you can safely trust one other member to be reasonable. If so, be sure he or she is willing to let you ultimately make the final decisions about what stays and what goes. This means that *you* will be making decisions for the rest of the family. This is a big responsibility with liability because you will hear about how you have emotionally damaged your family by throwing out some of their most prized possessions. Trust me, they will recover if you have done your job well with reflective consideration.

> When tackling a big project, you need to consider whether enlisting family members will help or hinder the process.

I wish my mother had taken this approach with my stuff. Instead, about six months after I married, she and Dad drove up for a visit with a U-Haul trailer tagging behind. The trailer was filled with everything I had left in their home. It held an amazing array of items going back to my early childhood. It included items such as gray boots with silver buckles from eighth grade, old prom dresses, posters, dead flowers, and all the artwork I ever produced. Of course, I threw out most of it. It's easy not to be sentimental when you are faced with a trailer full of stuff!

SEVEN STEPS TO FREEDOM

Of all the methods for sorting, the best ones always involve the use of boxes. Some methods say start with three: trash, keep, sell. However, I have found that four or more can be even more effective. Jeff Campbell in his book *Clutter Control* recommends seven. Here is his list:

1. Trash
2. Garage sale or charity
3. Belongs elsewhere
4. Not sure
5. Return to owner
6. Repair
7. Alter or mend

His method keeps the process moving forward because it allows you to postpone difficult decisions. Rather than get stuck, you simply place them in the *Not Sure* box. When I was moving out of my home after a difficult divorce, my friend Jan was there to postpone the pain of dealing with photos. She simply packed them away and moved them to a safe place in my new apartment to be dealt with later. Jeff Campbell's system also makes it easy to just drop that long lost baseball glove into the *Belongs Elsewhere* box rather than relocate it immediately. The most important thing to remember is that if you don't make some hard decisions as you sort, you can risk having as much stuff when you are finished as you had when you started.

GARAGE CENTRAL

Why is it that everything but the car seems to reside in the garage? The answer is that it is simply easier to drop stuff there than to carry it into the house. I did a segment for the television show *Mission Organization* on garage organizing. The family had a three-car garage that was so full of stuff there wasn't room for even one car. I started by zoning the spaces within the garage. The breadwinner for this family is the mom. She works as a dental sales representative, which means she must maintain inventory, ship product to dentists, and handle returns. She had inventory, boxes, and shipping materials all over the floor. She had no place to sit to organize and enter data into her laptop. So the first thing I did was plan for a shipping-and-receiving area that included a desk. They have two young children with bikes, trikes, toys, shoes, boots, and assorted backpacks. In addition, her husband likes to tinker with cars and that requires a ton of tools, car-care products, and an air compressor. Of course, no garage could be complete without the normal yard and garden equipment, including a small riding mower.

> Don't forget a locked cabinet to keep children and pets safe from toxic materials.

They were fortunate because I knew I would be able to get a garage organizing system donated as a trade for free national TV exposure. I called GarageTek because they have the most amazing system. They attach slotted panels to your walls to which you can attach a myriad of shelves, cabinets, hooks, and brackets for holding absolutely anything you need. When they were finished, the garage was designed with areas for the mother's office and inventory, the children's things (at a height they could easily reach), a garden center, and the last bay was reserved for her husband's hobby with cars. There was so much room that, believe it or not, all three cars fit into the garage as well.

You can make your garage well-organized by using any number of shelves and cabinets. There are so many different products available that are specifically designed for this use. The main point here is that you need to get items off the floor; once they start spreading across the floor it becomes impossible to keep them under control. And be sure to include a locking cabinet to keep children and pets safe from any toxic stuff, including household cleaning products.

ATTICS AND BASEMENTS

The biggest problem with attics and basements is that they can be damp, dark, hot, cold, and, unfortunately, out of sight. If it's out of sight, it's probably out of mind as well, which means you are likely not using most of what is stored there. You know you are really in trouble if the stairs leading down to these spaces are so cluttered you cannot get past. This would be the place to begin, by making your pathway clear and safe.

Once you can actually get into your attic or basement, evaluate your lighting situation. If it's too dark to see what you have in there, you will need to add lighting before you begin reorganizing. If it's damp, you will need to address this issue as well. I chose to add a dehumidifier to my basement. I use it year-round; I change the setting to absorb more moisture in the summer and less in the winter. It retrieves over two gallons of water a day during the summer. That's a lot of water that could otherwise be a major cause of damage. I also added a sump pump to avoid any problems from flooding.

The number one rule (that we all break) is: Never use cardboard boxes to store anything in a space that is damp. You will only be asking for trouble such as mold, mildew, bugs, and smelly destruction. I could not locate the source of a horrible smell in my basement. It went on for two months. It was awful. You know what it was? It was a large insect that chose to die in a storage area near the bathroom. It was amazing how it stank. Once removed, the smell was gone. An activated charcoal filter is a good way to eliminate an unwanted odor caused by dampness.

> An activated charcoal filter is a good way to eliminate an unwanted odor caused by dampness.

SIMPLICITY MADE SIMPLE

GET YOUR BOXES OFF THE FLOOR and avoid stacks. Substitute shelves for stacks to allow airflow around boxes to keep mildew from growing.

Use rigid clear plastic storage boxes and be sure to **LABEL EVERYTHING**. Also include location guides on all labels. You will always be assured that everyone in the family will be able to return items after use if you simply mark the front of your shelves with the name of the box.

Location, location, location. It's true in real estate and it's true for your storage real estate. Take the time to **ZONE EACH AREA OF YOUR STORAGE SPACE**. Create zones such as holiday items, out-of-season clothing, sports equipment, gardening, hobbies, and so forth.

Think about reaching high places and **USE ALL YOUR VERTICAL SPACE**. Purchase a sturdy step stool for *each* area of storage. I even have one in my closet because it makes it easier for me to use the higher shelves. Be sure to place the *most used* items at your waist level to make them easy to reach. Place the items that are *least used* at the highest level because they will require the use of the step stool. Place the rest below waist level.

IF SOMETHING IS CONSIDERED HAZARDOUS, then you probably shouldn't be storing it at all. If you must store flammables such as gasoline and paint thinner, the garage is the better choice. Rid your home of any paint or oil-stained rags. To dispose of these items, place them into a tin can with a lid.

POWER TOOLS are a magnet for budding home remodelers. Be sure to keep them safely locked away.

EXTREME TEMPERATURES can make any of these places the wrong place to store paints, crafts, or garden supplies. A simple way to find out your climate situation is hang a thermometer and check it often. Be sure to read labels to determine ideal storage locations.

Lord, only You know what is hidden
in the secret places of my life. Cleanse me from
inside out so that I can stand unashamed
in the face of each new day. Create in me a right heart
that stays on a straight path to Your perfect plan.

Cyclical Chaos

The Israelites did evil in the eyes of the Lord;

they forgot the Lord their God and served

the Baals and the Asherahs.

—JUDGES 3:7 (NIV)

The book of Judges is about sin and its consequences. It describes an ongoing cycle of peace, followed by complacency, which leads to sin accompanied with pain, causing the people to cry out to God. God rescues them, which results in peace, and the cycle repeats itself, on and on and on. What would it take for the people to learn?

One answer to their prayer was a judge named Deborah. Now she was not a woman you would want to reckon with—she could really hold her own against evil forces. She is the judge who finally broke the cycle and led the Israelites against the Canaanite King Jabin, freeing Israel of foreign oppression for forty years.

Too often, we get caught in similar cycles in our lives. Without realizing it, we become the cause of our chaos. Somehow, some way, we seem to think that even if we keep doing things the same way, they will suddenly change. Logically, we know this isn't true, yet we continue. Why is it we keep falling into the same trap? Just like the Israelites, we find that staying in a rut is simpler than making changes.

The Israelites worshipped Baal because there were idols of Baal on every street corner. That was certainly easier than going to the temple. The Baal idols were obvious and attractive. The easy way is always attractive, but that doesn't make it right—or make it work.

> Often without realizing it, we become the cause of our own chaos.

GET RID OF USELESS ITEMS!

I was having a discussion with a client recently about the care of aging relatives and their homes. I was telling her about my aunt who left the family with a house literally full of stuff. I am not exaggerating when I say you could not walk through this house. How my aunt managed, I will never know. It was so sad and so filthy. The family tried for the last several years of her life to help clean. She refused. Eventually, she simply refused to allow us into her home for any occasion. We knew it was going to be bad when she died, but it was worse than we imagined.

My client has a similar situation brewing with her mother. How do you prevent it? For her mom, like my aunt, it had reached the point of no return. Trust me, you do not want to leave this kind of mess as your legacy. If you are heading in this direction, now is the time to turn things around.

In order to manage the chaos in your home you must repent from your old way of doing things. You must learn, for example, to say no to all those beautiful and artistically enchanting ads for evermore magazine subscriptions. How many do you subscribe to now? How many of them are you actually reading?

Speaking of reading, how many books promising to make you thinner, healthier, wiser, richer, and prettier have you bought? How many have you read enough of to even benefit from?

Unfortunately, our good intentions can lead to more clutter and junk mail in our homes. And since we paid good money for all of our things, we are unwilling to simply throw them out. It does you no good to be faithful to those dollars spent on things you will not use. Just for the record, keeping them is not an example of good stewardship.

Are you a coupon clipper with good intentions? In order for the coupons to be of benefit, they must be easily found when you are ready to go shopping. I save about ten to fifteen dollars every week. It's not a lot, but it is enough over the course of a month to go out to dinner on.

I keep my coupon process simple. I have a box in the drawer below my kitchen phone where I drop the coupons. Knowing the newest ones are on top, I always start searching from the bottom of the pile. No filing, no mess, and I always know where they are.

> In order to manage the chaos in your home, you must learn to say no.

As an interior designer, I am one of the few professionals that really see the inside of closets. I do know what you have in there—and it's not a pretty sight. If you frequently find yourself shopping at the clothing outlet rather than selecting clothes from your closet, something must be seriously wrong. If there is nothing in your closet that you want to wear, you either have an addiction to shopping, are afraid to wear the same thing twice, or you need to throw out everything in your closet. It may be that you bought things because they were on sale instead of investing in something that you love. If you don't break this cycle, your closet will continue to fill with clothes you refuse to wear.

Do you see a cyclical pattern to your behavior? Must I call Judge Deborah or the Style Police? The sad thing is that many of us fall prey to this deception. We hold out hope that our bodies will once again be able to wear those tiny little clothes that we spent a fortune on ten years ago. Sorry friends, we all must face reality. Even if by some miracle we were to slim down to those long-ago sizes, the clothes will not be in style. And if they are—we will definitely be too old to wear them.

PUT YOUR LIFE IN ORDER

I believe that if your house is not in order, your life probably is not either. Making significant changes to eliminate the chaos of your home begins with making a personal choice. First, realize that you *are* in charge. I know it may not feel like it but the state of your home and your life has everything to do with the choices you are making every day. The problem often is that you are reacting to life rather than taking charge of it.

> If your house is not in order, your life probably is not either.

When I talk with people about their homes, I repeatedly hear similar statements: Life is just too busy to find time to do things differently. I agree that life is too busy. Everyone I speak with feels the same way. But only you can change that. Only you can cut activities from your schedule to allow time for life's priorities.

Most of us come from two-income families. Many others are single parents. And as statistics prove, all of us are working more hours than ever before. I was dismayed to read recently that France has decided to give up on its thirty-five-hour workweek. They have given in and accepted the reality that to compete in a global society, they must begin to work the longer workweek of the rest of the developed world. This saddened me because I have long believed they had it right. They worked to live, not lived to work.

The first thing that must be addressed then is finding more time. Small changes can have a big impact here. By simply arranging to share babysitting with a friend one night a week, you can gain invaluable time for yourself. You can choose to use those hours however you wish. Make sure your spouse is on board for this arrangement and is willing to fetch his or her own dinner. This is your time!

I believe a little self-care is the best way to start. Self-care is also about caring for your soul. You will not be able to make yourself whole if your spiritual well-being is not being nurtured and fed. A renewed spirit is the perfect encouragement for new directions. Once your head and your heart are clear and strong, it's time to dig in and make some new choices for the management of your home.

Lack of time is not the only thing that prevents us from moving forward with good choices. Sometimes we create ways to avoid the work. For example, rather than attack your closet, you decide the car needs washing, or you have to return all the e-mails in your in-box, or you absolutely must call back that telemarketer and tell him to stop calling! This is called procrastination.

Although many think procrastination is a simple thing, in reality it is complex. It involves thoughts and attitudes that often we are not even aware of. Psychologist Clayton E. Tucker Ladd, in *Psychological Self-Help*, divides procrastinators into two categories: *afraid types* who are filled with self-doubt, low self-esteem and fear of failure; and *relaxer types* who are easily distracted by more pleasurable activities than the tasks that seem hatefully boring. In the end, much of our home chaos can be eliminated or pared down by making simple changes in our thought processes.

> Much of our home chaos can be eliminated by making simple changes in our thought processes.

SIMPLICITY MADE SIMPLE

BREAK UP LARGE PROJECTS INTO SMALLER TASKS. For example, cleaning your closet can be divided into: determining what is still in style and what's still in good shape, then trying on clothes to determine what fits.

TACKLE THE SHOES IN YOUR CLOSET USING THE SAME CRITERIA. Then, and only then, can you think organization. Perhaps it's time for a new closet organization system. It won't seem nearly so burdensome if you take a small bit at a time.

JUST DO IT! The next time you catch yourself saying, "I don't *feel* like doing this now, I can do this later," think Nike. If you force yourself to push through the negative emotion and move into action, you will probably feel much better when you are finished.

PLAN FOR FUN AND RELAXATION AS WELL AS WORK. I always write my *off* time as well as home tasks into my schedule. That way if I find myself thinking about things I would rather be doing as I work through my tasks, I am able to concentrate much more easily knowing I have scheduled time for fun. Besides, I enjoy my leisure time more because I don't have to feel guilty about the work not getting done.

CHANGE YOUR EXPECTATIONS. Perfectionism and feelings that things should be a certain way can be stumbling blocks. My assistant Patty was recently showing her young son how to separate the white from the yellow of an egg. He was excited and eager to learn. However, he decided that he knew a better way to do it. His idea was to make a hole in the bottom of the shell just large enough for the white to funnel out. His smart mom said, "Okay, let's try it." And it worked! Next time you catch yourself using language like "should" or "must," reevaluate. Perhaps you are actually creating roadblocks to getting the work done.

Lord, I repent of bad habits that reap
unpleasant results. I give you my old way
of thinking and ask that You renew my thoughts
to be in line with Your good plan for my life.

PART FIVE

Creating a Spiritual Sanctuary

HOME SHOULD ALWAYS represent a place of safety, a sanctuary where you can meet with God and the ones you love to be revived and restored. Even a simple, well-organized home sees difficult days, but there is a way to allow grace to carry you through the storms of life. In this last section, I will show you how to create your own special place to meet God, so that you will be ready to open your home to lift others. Enjoy!

The Abundant Life
Is Authentic Wealth

[Love] bears all things, believes all things,
hopes all things, endures all things.

—1 CORINTHIANS 13:7 (NKJV)

First Corinthians 13 is often called "The Love Chapter," and is frequently read at weddings. However, if you love anyone, you know that it's the daily part of living together *after* the wedding that gets hard.

As the above Scripture says, *love bears all things*. Sometimes it is the little annoyances that are most difficult to bear, such as someone leaving the cap off the toothpaste, turning the toilet paper roll differently than you prefer, or leaving dirty dishes in the sink too long. Do you love them enough to simply put up with these little things? Or will you waste years of joy by making a big deal out of the small issues every chance you get?

Love is to *believe all things*. Are you usually a trusting person? Are you able to think the best of those around you? More important, do you believe all of God's promises and trust Him completely? This is an especially good question to ask yourself as you and your spouse go head to head on what gets tossed from the garage. If you truly believe in your loved ones, then it means trusting them on the decisions they make. I know it can be hard as your husband attempts to convince you that he absolutely must have that two thousand-dollar wall-mounted HDTV. But he can't understand why you want to spend two thousand dollars to renovate the master bedroom.

Love *hopes all things*. Are you an optimist who expects good things to happen? Or do you let negative thoughts cause you to fear and fret? Stress, anxiety, and fear can easily contribute to household disorder—both emotional and physical. I have seen parents who keep their children from learning basic life skills, like cooking and cleaning, because they fear for their children's safety. It's one thing to have justifiable concern; it's another to be so afraid that it immobilizes you. If stress, fear, or anxiety is creating chaos in your home, it is critical that you address those things that are at the root of your emotional disorder. Only then will you be able to handle the work of cleaning up the physical disorder in your home.

> Stress, anxiety, and fear can easily contribute to household disorder— both emotional and physical.

Love *endures all things*. Do you love enough to endure miserable situations? There are phases and stages to all of life. Some of those stages can create a miserable situation. If you do not have a strong spiritual foundation, as well as a strong home foundation, it can be extremely difficult to get through life's tough times. Financial struggles, health issues, even aging parents can test your endurance. Sometimes, the best way to get through these tough times is simply to accept them. It's easy to fall into an attitude of resistance, rather than just accept reality. Often the situation is temporary and it is best to let it run its course.

RECEIVE GRACE FOR DIFFICULT DAYS

Attitude and perspective are two tools that we all have that can completely change our outlook and ability to endure hard situations. One client, in particular, has had what I consider to be an extremely difficult year. First came the call from paramedics saying that her twenty-five-year-old son was just rushed to a hospital. He was in a coma from a drug overdose. This was a dedicated young Christian man. No one even suspected he was using drugs. The doctors encouraged her to pull his life-line on three separate occasions. As a mother, she refused. She promised God that if he lived she would spend the rest of her life taking care of him.

> The goal for our homes should be to create an atmosphere that reflects God's kind of love.

Within months, her husband lost his job. The only job he could find was a state away. That move took her far from her church, her support group, and her home. After a year and a half her son was finally released from the hospital. Although many would think this was time for celebration, the reality of caring for a completely paralyzed and blind grown son was harder than she ever imagined. Her *can do* attitude was soon falling prey to exhaustion, anger, and fear. And all of these were justifiable responses to an unusually difficult situation.

Nonetheless, it was these same three responses that compounded the problem. Her exhaustion, anger, and fear began to make her son feel even guiltier than he did before. His response was to try to ease her workload by demanding less, even when his need was critical. Her husband soon became an easy target for her growing anger. The home situation was certainly deteriorating.

Eventually, her sweet son asked her to pray with him. As they began daily prayer—often three and four times a day—everyone's attitude and perspective improved. God is good. His love is abundant even for the toughest times of life. The good news for this family is that the love has never been sweeter.

God has provided a wonderful Christian caretaker two days a week to ease the burden. But even better news is that their son is beginning to get peripheral vision—and that is amazing.

The goal for our homes and those that reside in them should be to create an atmosphere that reflects God's kind of love. That's not to say that loving God's way is easy: It's not. But when we surrender to Him and love Him with all our hearts, He will strengthen us. There have been days when I have literally prayed for God to give me His love for family members, recognizing that at that particular moment I was not capable of loving them on my own.

SIMPLICITY MADE SIMPLE

Accept the fact that we are weak and far from perfect, but **WE CAN DEPEND ON GOD**—no matter what!

Someone has said that when God makes a promise, faith believes it, hope anticipates it, and patience quietly awaits it. Bill Gothard defines patience as "accepting a difficult situation without giving God a deadline to remove it." **GOD MOVES IN HIS OWN TIME**, in His own way. While we wait, the Holy Spirit will guide us and we need not fear.

SOMETIMES GOD HAS TO SLOW US DOWN or stop us before he can get through to us. There are many prisoners who have said, "If I hadn't been arrested and sent here, drugs probably would have killed me by now." I am sure you have heard stories of broken engagements that later led to the brokenhearted finding their true soul mate. I believe that we always have a choice. We have the choice to allow the bad times to either make us bitter or make us better. You decide.

Troubles always seem magnified in the dark. That makes the night the best time to pray. **PRAYER CAN BRING PEACE** to our hearts and minds as it reminds us that God is in charge and that He can keep us safe. Surrender your worries to Him. As you pray—be sure to stretch out your arms and hold your hands with palms *down*. That way you cannot close your palms and hold on to your worries. Instead, your cares will fall from your hands. This will be a simple symbolic gesture that your worries are all in His hands and you can move on.

EVERYONE NEEDS TIME FOR HIMSELF OR HERSELF. But too often, we plan how we want to spend our free time and neglect to communicate our plans to the rest of the family. I am very disciplined, which makes it hard for me to be spontaneous. With a busy schedule and tight deadlines, I have to plan each day of the week. The sad and difficult result is that if my husband comes to me and says, "It's a beautiful day, let's go play golf," I usually feel as though I can't because my schedule doesn't permit. I know I can't plan for that unexpected beautiful day, but I need to learn to plan more flexibility in my schedule. And my husband needs to learn to plan in advance better. That way, we are respecting each other's time and needs.

> Heavenly Father, strengthen my love
> so that I love others as You love me.
> Give me patience to wait for Your answers.

Creating a Spiritual
Sanctuary in Your Home

Thought is the wind, knowledge the sails and

mankind the vessel. . . . And home the sanctuary.

—AUGUST HARE (1792–1834)

Holy . . . what does that word mean to you? Is it awesome, reverent, and peaceful? The Bible says the saints are holy. Of course, we know that God is holy. But what about your home? Is it holy? It should be. The above quotation inspires us to make our homes holy unto the Lord. I know from experience that if we sanctify our homes to the Lord, then they will also be a sanctuary for us.

Home sanctuaries are as unique as the individuals who reside in them. For some city dwellers, the hustle-bustle urban energy is what makes their home a sanctuary. They can enjoy the beauty and solitude of the country—but only for a short time. Within a few days they are ready to run back to the city. I used to be a city girl, but I am a convert after living in the country for nearly twenty-four years. Now when I visit the big city, I can't wait to get home.

I am often asked by people to help them create sanctuary spaces. Some ask for a prayer closet. Others want to transform an entire room to be used as their place of quiet and solitude. Yet others would like their family room to evoke a sense of spiritual holiness. Sarah Ban Breathnach wrote in her best-selling book *Simple Abundance* how she realized one day that she spent most of her time reading in the bedroom—away from her family. But it wasn't by choice. She discovered that although her husband and her daughter had comfortable places to sit in the family room, she did not. She had designed herself out of the comfort of enjoying quiet time with her family. Unless we make a conscious effort to create sanctuaries within our homes, they won't happen.

CREATE A SPACE IN WHICH TO MEET WITH GOD

In designing the perfect sanctuary you must first understand your personal spiritual style. My friend Jan is a dancer and choreographer; it is not unusual for her to meet God in the midst of working on a dance piece. Since her focus of study and teaching is sacred dance, it is only natural for sacred music to be part of her spiritual experience. A spiritual sanctuary for her might be a large open room or a field filled with wildflowers—anywhere she can worship God in dance.

> Your spiritual sanctuary needs to speak to your own spiritual style.

I grew up living only blocks from the water. Sitting on the rocks as the water lapped up to the shore was where I most often found myself when I needed to talk to God. I have attempted to make my entire home a spiritual sanctuary by including those things that remind me of the sea.

My personal sanctuary space changes with the seasons. In the warm summer months, my screened porch is the place that I naturally gravitate to for alone time with God. Simple reminders from the shore help me quickly find that place of peace. On my wicker table I have an oil candle that I made from a small old green-glass bottle. With the oil I mixed tiny shells—their simple miniature beauty amazes me. Only God could make something so small and beautiful. My friend Jan gave me a hand-made green pottery bowl with a heart-shaped cutout. In it, shells and small pieces of driftwood surround a pillar candle.

In the cold winter months, my favorite chair sits next to a basket where I keep my Bible, prayer journal, and current reading material. As I snuggle under the wraps of a soft woven throw, it is easy for me to simply find time for solitude with God. Even with my busy life, it is easy for me to find time because everything I need is already conveniently where I need it.

Often the bathroom is the place where we can most easily drift into quiet peace. My mother has always used the bathroom as her sanctuary. Every evening, like clockwork, Mom closes the door and runs herself a warm soothing bath with her favorite scented oil. With six children at home, that half-hour, late-evening ritual used to be the only time Mom had for herself. Now she continues to use this as her time alone with God. Her bathroom walls are decorated with the soft pastels of pale orchid, green, peach and white wall covering. Although her bathroom is small, it is beautiful, which just proves that no matter how the bath industry tries to lure you into spending thousands of dollars to create a sanctuary, it is not necessary. A few lush towels and a soft bath mat can graciously be all the comfort you need for sanctuary.

The key for creating your personal sanctuary is finding elements that inspire

> Try a little music in your sanctuary. But listen to music that moves you, rather than music thought to be soothing.

your senses to recall a place that most reminds you of holiness. That is why scented candles are often a part of a sanctuary space. For me, candles that smell of the ocean immediately take me to my sanctuary by the sea where I have always found it easy to commune with God. Perhaps your strongest sense is touch; in that case find a soft comforting pillow or throw.

Symbols also play a big part in drawing nearer to our Creator. My assistant Patty keeps a small piece of coal in her jewelry box. It came from one of the sermons our pastor gave as a reminder of how we are works in progress. The ugly little piece of coal over time will be transformed into a beautiful diamond. For Patty, it is a concrete reminder that although she is in progress, God is loving her through the journey. It allows her to have grace to accept herself as God accepts her. This makes it easier for her to be in the presence of God without feeling unworthy.

Light is another effective tool for creating a sanctuary. I love the warmth and glow of sunshine. An abundance of daylight and a soothing palette of colors and textures are the ultimate relaxation for people like me. For others, the stillness of night may be more calming. I find rippling water to be visually calming and almost spiritually nurturing. That is why I have incorporated a fountain that can be heard throughout the house in the foyer of my home.

SIMPLICITY MADE SIMPLE

BEGIN by finding a space that looks, feels, and smells right to you. Clean the room well: this is your purifying act. Be sure you have the appropriate lighting for your own comfort level. Then gather all the items that will help to make your space sacred. These may include candles, symbols, books, pillows, photos, or flowers. The goal is to create a space that gives you an overall sense of peace.

YOU DON'T NEED A LOT OF ROOM for your sanctuary. Small intimate spaces can make it easy to embrace holiness. One client uses her laundry room as her sanctuary. We added a small desk with hanging wood files along the wall to hold her necessary reading materials. We added a beautiful fabric skirt to her utility tub to simply make it pretty.

FIND A CORNER AND MAKE IT YOUR OWN. For one client we stole away a corner in the bedroom. A comfy chair, a soft throw, and pretty pillow, combined with baskets and a reading lamp, were all she needed. Whenever she finds fifteen minutes in her schedule, she simply hides away by closing the bedroom door and turning off the ringer on her bedroom telephone.

If you love the outdoors, then you may find quiet places that can become **YOUR OUTDOOR SANCTUARIES**. Pay attention to places that nourish your soul. For me, a walk along the beach is perfect. Perhaps you love the mountains. Then taking a hike with God's mountain creatures and creation can be your personal outdoor sanctuary.

As your **LIFE CHANGES**, so too may your personal sanctuary. Allow yourself the freedom to change your space or spaces as you grow and change. There are no hard and fast rules. It is all about knowing yourself and finding a place that allows you to be closer to God. Finding a place where you feel comfortable enough to be honest with Him. It should be a place where your soul longs to be—a little heaven on earth.

Choose your **PERSONAL SPIRITUAL PRACTICE**. If music stirs your heart toward God, then make it a part of your sanctuary. My friend Lynn Morrisey journals her prayers. Her book *Love Letters to God* is an amazing expression of love and a tool for growing closer to our Creator. Her personal sanctuary always includes a beautiful journal and pen. These are critical elements to her prayer life.

Lord, I want to be closer to You. As I look
at a spectacular sunset or climb the high mountains,
I am reminded of all Your glory. Hear my prayer
to join me in my sanctuary, so I may hear
Your voice and feel Your awesome presence.

Hospitality Is
Spiritually Fulfilling

Martha was distracted by all the preparations that

had to be made. . . . the Lord answered, "you are worried

and upset about many things, but only one thing

is needed. Mary has chosen what is better,

and it will not be taken away from her."

—LUKE 10:40–42 (NIV)

This familiar passage of Scripture sums up all we really need to know about hospitality. Still, many of us get so caught up in cleaning, preparation, and serving that we are either unable to entertain at all, or when we do, we neglect our guests. Our personalities have a lot to do with our ability to enjoy the pleasure of entertaining people in our homes.

Some people simply aren't comfortable in social situations, so they immerse themselves in preparations. Keeping yourself busy in the kitchen can be a way to avoid the uneasiness of the situation, but it also means you miss the blessing of community. Our personality traits, unfortunately, can also affect our ability to truly commune with God. It's easy to get so busy doing things *for* Him, that we aren't spending any time *with* Him.

A dear elderly saint of a woman, Dottie Omundsen, who lives here in Lancaster, Pennsylvania, is the most gracious host. Her words of wisdom regarding hospitality and entertaining say it best, "If you've come to see *me*—come anytime. If you've come to see my home—call ahead." If only we could make everyone understand this message.

SHARE YOUR SANCTUARY WITH OTHERS

God designed us for community, and what better way to enjoy the fellowship of community than in our homes? I like to think of our homes the way the early Christians did—as a church. When you enter your church foyer, do you first look to see whether the vacuum was just run? Probably not. Instead, you focus on greeting old friends and introducing yourself to new ones. The same is usually true for those that we invite into our homes. Yes, we all know someone who focuses on the wrong things, but such people are in the minority. The easiest way to deal with them is to give them grace and not take their comments to heart. Romans 12:13 encourages us all to practice hospitality, whether it is our spiritual gift or not. The Greek word for hospitality, *philoxenia*, is actually a combination of two words: *philos*, meaning "loving," and *xenos,* meaning "a stranger."

I love the verse from Hebrews 13:2 (KJV) that says, "Be not forgetful to entertain strangers: for thereby some have entertained angels unawares." Wouldn't it be amazing to get to heaven and find out that you, in fact, had entertained an angel? I think one of the keys to successful hospitality is to be yourself, and entertain in a style that is most comfortable for you. Consider realistically your family and lifestyle, and don't set yourself up for disappointment. If you're really a chili person, then don't try to serve a seven-course fancy meal. Serve chili out of a bucket instead! Tell everyone to come in jeans, and enjoy yourself.

Isn't Christianity supposed to be the life of open hands, open hearts, and open doors? When we open our hearts as well as our homes, we're practicing Christianity in the form of hospitality. It's always important to keep our eye on the goal. The goal should be to spend quality time with people we love, or to show love to people we don't know.

I often find myself reminding people to enjoy the process of decorating because many approach it like a "job," and one they don't particularly enjoy. Entertaining can be just as daunting. But if you keep focused on the results, it makes the process easier. If not, then something is wrong. Either you're expecting too much from yourself, or you've chosen the wrong time to do it.

Just this morning I visited with a client whose home is *in process*. The draperies were just installed yesterday, so we can finally begin to add the most per-

> When we open our hearts as well as our homes, we're practicing Christianity in the form of hospitality.

sonal touches with accessories. I expected her to be excited because a dear friend was coming to visit that night from Kansas. When I arrived, she wasn't in the best of moods. There were many reasons for her somber mood, but one was the fact that her family room didn't look finished without accessories, and it was too late to go shopping that day.

In an attempt to make her smile and add a little fun to her weekend, I decided to go on an in-house scavenger hunt for things to temporarily fill the empty spaces. First, I spotted a rooster sitting in a dark corner on the kitchen counter. He fit perfectly on the mantel with three narrow wood candlesticks. Then I grabbed a crystal vase filled with vivid yellow gladiolas from her garden. It added the height and color we needed for the left side of the mantel. The fluted wood bowl filled with fresh bright yellow lemons was the perfect complement to the gladiolas. A wooden artichoke and a silver platter finished the composition. In the basement, I found yet another smaller rooster that now sits proudly on a stack of books on the sofa table, alongside a plant and a small white pitcher. By the time I finished, my client was smiling. She couldn't resist the rooster brigade; they added just the right amount of color and whimsy. There was also an unexpected blessing: it turns out the rooster on the mantel was a gift from her soon-to-arrive Kansas City friend. Wouldn't she be surprised!

Today's business climate often makes it necessary for us to entertain co-workers and associates. This can be especially nerve-wracking for everyone if it involves a spouse's business partners. A few simple considerations can go a long way to making even these situations successful. As always, the most important aspect should be the people. Many entertaining experts suggest planning around one *key guest*. Give him or her a few dates to choose from, then invite people who would interact well with the key guest. These are people whose personalities your key guest would enjoy or who might be of professional help to him or her. Fill the remaining seats with friends with whom you yourself like to spend time. This will take the edge off and give you a level of comfort as well as an extra pair of hands if you need them.

Nothing can help you find more joy in cooking meals and turning your household chores into a labor of love than the expectation of serving God. As Kathy Chapman Sharp explains, "The Book of First John makes it plain that when we love others, we are showing our love for God. He loves us completely and unconditionally. Equally, when we love and serve others in the community through hospitality, we are also serving God. That's the moment when your home becomes a sanctuary for those God sends your way."

SIMPLICITY MADE SIMPLE

PRACTICE MAKES PERFECT. Never attempt a new recipe without practicing first. My recommendation is go with whatever you cook best. You can always do what I do: Use fancy silver to serve everyday meals, then everyday becomes special. Practice makes perfect also holds true for all entertaining. The more you do it, the easier it gets.

You can't please everyone. As long as you are doing your best you are probably doing fine. The key is to **SET REALISTIC EXPECTATIONS** for yourself rather than try to meet those of relatives, friends, and foes.

A little **ORCHESTRATION** of the social dynamics can make the evening more pleasant for everyone. To accomplish this best, you determine where everyone should sit. For example, it makes sense to place a conversationalist with a "quiet type." By simply placing talkers with nontalkers you allow everyone to use his or her strengths.

DON'T put all the hors d'oeuvres in one place. Whenever I entertain, I make sure to have different food items placed throughout the house. This keeps the traffic moving and prevents any one room from getting overcrowded.

Remember Dottie Omundsen's advice and **DON'T WORRY TOO MUCH ABOUT CLEANING.** Your friends love you regardless. Besides, if it's too clean, people will be afraid to get comfortable.

SOME OF THE BEST get-together dinners have been spontaneous potlucks because we each contribute the items that we make best. I always get asked to bring my special salad. If we are grilling, then everyone knows to bring whatever main course item they want to have grilled. If you love steak, then bring your own steak;

if it's chicken, then go for it. This makes it not only easy for the host, but it's affordable as well.

ENJOY! As German author Jean Paul Richter (1763–1825) said, "The test of pleasure is the memory it leaves behind." I can guarantee you this: If you don't have fun, neither will your guests.

Father, thank You for putting people in my life whom I can enjoy entertaining in my home. Teach me to do the thing that is important when I entertain these guests—to love them on Your behalf.

A Gentle-Spirited Home

And my people shall dwell in a peaceable habitation,
and in sure dwellings, and in quiet resting places.

—ISAIAH 32:18 (KJV)

Creating a home that exudes a spirit of gentleness, compassion, and acceptance begins by nurturing a spiritual attitude for all of life. In a way, it's like looking at life through rose-colored glasses. A good attitude allows us to view everything from a spiritual perspective. Joy or suffering suddenly takes on a deeper meaning if we realize that everything is part of our educational experience for developing godly character. Through faith we are able to relax, breathe easier, trust, and be free from fear. A right spiritual attitude combined with faith will allow us to share our homes and ourselves without feeling insecure or overburdened.

Elizabeth Sherrill shares her story of the "Daylily Principle":

The daylilies are in bloom along our road, lifting their orange trumpets in joyous profusion. More than a blaze of color, for me they carry a message.

It was my friend Margaret Henrichsen who taught me to read it. Margaret was a widow in her sixties who stopped by our two-room apartment when I was a young mother. "There's no place to put things," I said, apologizing for the clutter. Baby bottles and children's toys competed for space with boxes of keepsakes—menus, travel souvenirs, theater programs, mementos of high school and college.

Margaret looked around for a place to set her coffee cup. "Tib," she said gently, "when you hold on to all these things, is it, perhaps, because you're afraid there won't be other exciting times?"

She paused while truth made its slow progress from the ear to the heart. "Your life won't always be diapers and piles of ironing, you know. There will be other trips, other adventures. You don't have to hoard the high spots. There will always be new ones."

She thought of it, she said, as the "Daylily Principle." "God never made a more glorious flower," she explained. "Yet each one, in all its perfection, lasts only a single day. God doesn't have to preserve it just because it's beautiful. He makes another one just as beautiful in its place."

Four decades have passed since Margaret's visit, and the adventure and variety she promised have come in abundance. I still keep reminders of special times—for a while. And when I need to let them go, I remember the daylilies and look forward to the new beauties that will unfold tomorrow.

It is this attitude that encourages us to enjoy all the things we have without becoming addicted to them. With this new freedom, we can enjoy all the blessings of life including family, friends, and home more abundantly. Ultimately, the spirit of our homes will be a reflection of our own spiritual attitude.

SIMPLICITY CREATES AN INVITING OASIS

If we fret and fray over our homes and the things within them to such a degree that our families cannot be comfortable, imagine how our guests will feel. The opposite can also be true. If you do not take enough pride in your home or yourself to be sure it is clean and comfortable, then this too is displeasing not only to your guests but also to God. Can you imagine your shock if, as you entered the pearly gates, you found it to be a chaotic mess, with smelly socks and dirty dishes?

As we seek to make our lives simpler and more balanced, we can look forward to the blessings that will come. Our personal sense of peace will translate to our daily living and our ability to open our homes by making them spiritual havens for all who enter. It is only when we can welcome our friends, as well as our family, with the same attitude that God welcomes us (sin and all) that our homes will truly be restful and peaceable dwellings that are safe and secure not only from the troubles outside, but also safe and secure emotionally, physically, and spiritually.

> Instead of focusing on your shortcomings, or the shortcomings of your home, consider those things that you do best.

> The holiest sanctuary is the home. The family altar is more venerable than that of a cathedral. The education of the soul for eternity should begin and be carried on at the fireside.
> —Richard Baxter, Puritan evangelist (1615–1691)

If Baxter was able to transform an entire town's attitude under his ministry, we should certainly be able to make a small difference within the ministry of our homes. When Baxter spoke of being reformed, he meant to be spiritually alive and morally in shape. This is a wonderful goal for our lives as well as our homes. God is compassionate and forgiving. We should not only have compassion and offer forgiveness to friends and family, but also to ourselves as well. Too often, we are so hard on ourselves that we are unable to see all that we do well.

Instead of focusing on your shortcomings, or the shortcomings of your home, consider those things that you do best. A friend once chastised me as I fretted about a particular area of weakness. She said that God had already forgiven me. If I could not forgive myself, then I was acting as though I was a higher authority than God was. That certainly put me straight. Who was I to question God's authority? If He had forgiven me, then it was done—simple as that.

As we all seek shelter from the storms brewing around the globe, our homes can be the sweetest harbor this side of heaven.

SIMPLICITY MADE SIMPLE

TAKE A FEW MINUTES to ponder these questions: How does your home feel? Is it warm and inviting? How does it make you feel and act the minute you get inside? Do you suddenly feel yourself getting angry or frustrated? Or do you let out a sigh of relief? How do you think visitors feel as they enter your home? Is it easy for them to find their way? Do they naturally gravitate to a specific room? Or are they outright overwhelmed and confused? Your answers will help you honestly evaluate the current attitude of your home.

LISTEN. What do you hear? This is one of the first things I pay attention to when I arrive at a new client's home. Noise can powerfully affect our emotional well-being. Over time, we learn to drown out those things we don't like, but that doesn't mean they are no longer there. Some sounds are soothing, such as the poetry of gurgling water. But listen carefully—is the sound of gurgling water coming from a tabletop fountain or a drippy faucet or leaky toilet?

As I work with clients to make their homes personal sanctuaries, I have found that the most aesthetically satisfying homes are those that engage all the senses. **HOW DOES YOUR HOME SMELL?** I have two cats, so I pay particular attention to be sure that the unpleasant smell of cat food isn't the first odor I notice. I have found that by simply leaving the window slightly open, there is enough ventilation to solve the problem.

CONSIDER blessing your home. The idea of the blessing is God's. The simple service of consecration with holy water, oils and incense is symbolic of the cleansing water of baptism. By setting apart our homes to be places wherein God is pleased to dwell, we ask for God's grace and presence in our daily lives. This surrendering of our spaces leads us to spiritual associations and awareness in all the places we go, not just the church.

> Father, I pray that our home will be filled
> with the fullness of Your presence and that all
> who enter may feel welcomed by it.
> May our love increase and overflow toward You,
> one another, and everyone else. May every activity
> that takes place in this home bring You glory.

Enjoy the Sabbath

"Remember the Sabbath day, to keep it holy."

—EXODUS 20:8 (NKJV)

God commanded a Sabbath because we need to spend unhurried time in worship and rest each week. Our sweet Lord cares not only about our spiritual well-being, but also our physical well-being. He is concerned enough to provide a full day each week for simple wonderful rest. In Old Testament times, the Sabbath day served to remind each generation of Israelites of their roots and their identity as God's covenantal people. It commemorated not only the seventh day of creation week but also God's deliverance of Israel from slavery in Egypt. The act of the Hebrew people resting from ordinary labor also served as a symbol of God's covenant with Israel.

Unfortunately, by Jesus' time the general prohibition against work on the Sabbath had been greatly exaggerated. The Law of His time included thirty-nine major forbidden activities, many of them so ridiculous that simply pulling a few ears of wheat was outlawed. This is what caused the conflict between Jesus and the Pharisees as told in

Matthew 12. As Lord of the Sabbath, Jesus reaffirmed the purpose of the Sabbath as a time for spiritual and physical renewal, reclaiming it from the overzealous legalists.

Jesus, through His sacrifice, ultimately fulfilled the keeping of the Sabbath. He is our Sabbath Rest. At one time, the Israelites looked to the serpent on the pole for physical healing (Numbers 21:8). This was merely a pattern to prepare them to look to Jesus on the cross for spiritual healing. This same lesson pattern is demonstrated in how the Israelites at one time observed the seventh day in honor of God's perfect creation, and in honor of God's power to save them from physical slavery. The early church quickly changed their Sabbath-keeping from the seventh day (our Saturday) to the first day (Sunday, often called "The Lord's Day"), because this was the day of the week on which our Savior rose from the dead. This biblically supports not only keeping the Sabbath but also the spiritual reality of Christ's redemption.

> The Sabbath is a time to focus on *being*, rather than *doing*.

Today the Christian day of worship, like the Jewish Sabbath, is a day to remember what God has done for us. It is not a day to be loaded down with obligations. As Christ instructed, it is a day of renewal, physically and spiritually. Our Sunday Sabbath is Christ's invitation to renew our personal relationship with Him and a time to celebrate the people in our lives. It is a time to focus on *being* instead of *doing*. It is about simplicity, which is an affair of the heart and an attitude of contentment.

IT'S A DAY GOD MADE FOR YOU

Learn to use the Sabbath day to take a break from the hustle and bustle of your life. Try something as simple as pulling out your lawn chairs and sitting with loved ones in the middle of the afternoon.

Van Varner wrote one of my favorite stories about rest:

Miss Belknap was my music teacher, and in me she had a pupil with neither eye nor ear for music. I'll not forget the day she tried to explain to me what a musical rest was. "This long dash," she said, "indicates a full measure of silence, and this shorter one is a half-measure." Then she went on to point out some little flaglike symbols that split the measure into various fractions ranging from quarters to sixty-fourths. "Now," she asked, "do you understand what a rest is?"

"Yes," I replied, "a rest is anything from a sixty-fourth to a full measure of nothing."

"Well, not exactly," she said. "A rest is not nothing. I mean, it is something, just as a silence is not nothing. Right?"

I looked at Miss Belknap blankly as she launched into a long lecture about how the rest was a rhythmic silence that the composer in his genius had placed there as part of the grand design of his work, and though the rest might seem like repose, it was really very busily working both for the composition and for the musician playing it. So now did I understand?

That was my last music lesson.

So I never learned to read music, but Miss Belknap's words caused me to muse about the kind of relaxation that most of us think about when we hear the word "rest."

Miss Belknap was right. A rest is not nothing. It is part of God's grand design both for Himself and for us. He gave us a full measure of it called the Sabbath.

What does Sabbath mean to you? For some it is a great way to escape housework. For others, it's a time to indulge in the pleasures they normally don't have time for, such as crafting, having brunch with friends, or simply hanging around. I may be considered strange, but one of my favorite Sunday pastimes is ironing.

Yes, I did say ironing. You see, I love having my bed linens ironed. I love the smell and feel of freshly laundered and ironed sheets. During my hectic week I never have time to iron. So on Sunday afternoon, I enjoy leisurely ironing my sheets with care. I put on my favorite music, set up my ironing board, and get to the pleasurable job of ironing. And I enjoy every minute of it!

> We are renewed physically and spiritually when we take time to rest and focus on God.

As you explore new ways and gain deeper meaning from keeping the Sabbath holy, don't get caught up in Old Testament legalism. As Jesus pointed out in Mark 2:27 (KJV), "The sabbath was made for man, and not man for the sabbath." Jesus also used the example of David going into the temple and eating the showbread (which was against the law) to point out how ridiculous the Pharisees' accusations of Jesus were regarding the Sabbath. God created the Sabbath for *our* benefit, not His own. God derives no benefit from us having a day of rest. We are restored and renewed physically and spiritually when we take time to rest and focus on God and others. It is critical to remember the real purpose and intent to truly benefit from the blessings of the Sabbath rest.

SIMPLICITY MADE SIMPLE

To encourage the celebration of family, recreate the old tradition of a **SUNDAY FAMILY MEAL**. Encourage all members to keep this as a date that holds priority in their life. For an alternative, try making Sunday evening a family game night.

Board games are cool again, and it's a great way to teach children the value of teamwork.

If you can manage time alone, **LET SUNDAY EVENING BE YOUR SPA NIGHT**. Allow yourself to indulge in a peaceful bubble bath while you play your favorite inspirational music softly in the background. Then listen carefully for the still small voice of your Lord to speak.

WHEN I WAS A KID, we either spent Sunday afternoons at Grandma's or we went for a drive in the country. It was a wonderful event with all eight of us piled into the old station wagon. We didn't have seat belts in those days; we hung out the back window and yet we all survived intact. Our favorite game was to see which of us children could convincingly act asleep so Dad would carry us from the car to our bed. Of course, he knew we were only pretending, but he went along with it to make our little dream come true.

Consider making Sunday your **FAMILY DAY FOR VOLUNTEERING**. My niece Gina loves elderly people. It is not uncommon for her to visit with patients at a nursing home. They love seeing her as much as she enjoys being there. Perhaps there is a widow or widower in your church who would love to be a part of your Sunday family dinner.

SPEND TIME OUTDOORS just enjoying nature or taking care of it. If you love gardening, then celebrate your freedom by tending to your garden. Remember that it's not about a list of things that you *can't* do—it's about doing things that renew you. Our society has lost the beauty of **A HANDWRITTEN LETTER**. Perhaps you can make Sunday your writing day. Imagine the joy that a handwritten letter will bring to the receiver. There's an added benefit for you too. While you write you will have the pleasure of reliving happy memories of the special things you and your friend experienced together. I recently received a card from my lifelong friend Krissy. In it she enclosed a three-page letter of wonderful shared memories. Now that's a great way to celebrate the Sabbath.

Lord, teach me to keep the Sabbath holy in Your eyes.
I am thankful that I can rest my life in Your hands.

Conclusion

I hope *The Simple Home* has helped you to discover your own creative style of decorating and inspired you to optimize the spiritual health and peacefulness of your home. If your heart is yearning for a simpler, more godly life that is filled with the people, activities, and things that you love, your home can be the place to start.

Create and keep a mission statement for your home that reflects the beauty and depth of our Lord's creation. Functionality combined with safety and comfort, while remaining gracious enough to soothe the senses and nourish dreams, is the best way to create an inviting home. The most aesthetically pleasing rooms employ all the elements that God has inspired: color, sound, scent, order, and beauty.

Especially consider beauty. We find real beauty in the acts of love that take place within our homes, as well as in the decorations that adorn our rooms. The life well lived brings the beauty that is key to our lasting happiness. Simply decorating with beautiful objects won't make us love our homes, but learning to focus on the good that happens in our homes will. I believe that conscious awareness of the beauty and joy of life is the first step in enhancing our lives.

Don't lose perspective on all the unfinished projects. Accept that even the simplest, most organized homes see difficult days, and realize that you are still in charge. I know that it may not always feel like it, but the state of your home and your life has everything to do with the choices you make each day. When you learn to take charge of life, rather than simply react to it, you will find peace within yourself and your home.

Remember, too, that a home is never really finished because the people living in it are continuously growing and changing. The key to a simple, friendly home lies in creating one that can adapt to change. Allow your home to grow with you, your family, and your life.

Creating a home that exudes a spirit of gentleness, compassion, and acceptance begins by nurturing a spiritual attitude for all of life. You can achieve this attitude by strengthening your connection to God, which helps you view everything from a spiritual perspective. Joy or suffering suddenly takes on a deeper meaning if you realize that everything you experience is part of a plan for developing your character.

Your goal is contentment. Being content, from a biblical perspective, means knowing that what you have is enough. Contentment is also a sense of freedom from too much reliance on other people or things. Learn to enjoy what you have, use it well as a blessing from God, and be patient regarding the ideas you have for your home. Maintaining a good attitude allows grace to carry you always, even through the storms of life.

Through faith we are able to relax, breathe easier, trust, and be free from fear. A right attitude combined with faith allows us to share our homes and our lives without feeling insecure or overburdened. Our homes should always represent a place of safety—a sanctuary where we can meet with God and the ones we love, and where we are revived and restored. The simple home is a harbor for a beautiful attitude within. Only houses that are filled with peace continue to beckon their owners to come home again and again.

Bibliography

Andrews, Cecile, *The Circle of Simplicity: Return to the Good Life* (New York: HarperCollins), 23.

Breathnach, Sarah Ban, *Simple Abundance: A Daybook of Comfort and Joy* (New York: Warner Books, 1995), May 21.

Campbell, Jeff, *Clutter Control: Putting Your Home on a Diet* (New York: Dell, 1992), 30–31.

Jones, Laurie Beth, *The Path: Creating Your Mission Statement for Work and for Life* (New York: Hyperion, 1996), xvii.

Judd, H. Stanley, *Think Rich* (New York: Delacorte Press, 1978).

Morgenstern, Julie, *Organizing from the Inside Out* (New York: Owl Books), 57–68.

Morrisey, Lynn D., *Love Letters to God: Deeper Intimacy through Written Prayer* (Sisters, Oregon: Multnomah Publishing, 2004).

Sharp, Kathy Chapman, "Christian Hospitality," *Christian Single* magazine (www.lifeway.com).

Stephens, Steve, *Lists to Live By for Simplicity* (Sisters, Oregon: Multnomah Publishers, Inc., 2002), 28.

Stoddard, Alexandra, *Creating a Beautiful Home* (New York: Avon Books/ William & Morrow, 1992).

Suchecka, Rysia, "Unexpected Acts of Kindness," *Contract* magazine (February 2004): 100.

Tedrick, Michael, *California Design Library—Bedrooms* (San Francisco: Chronicle Books, 1998), 54.

Tolpin, Judd, *The New Family Home: Creating the Perfect Home for Today and Tomorrow* (Newton, Connecticut: Taunton Press, 2000), 7.

Tucker-Ladd, Clayton E. *Psychological Self-Help* (Clayton Tucker-Ladd & Mental Health Net, 1996–2000), Chapter 4.

The Spirit of Simple Living™

by Sharon Hanby-Robie

The Simple Home

A Simple Christmas

The Spirit of Simple Living series offers uplifting titles that will help readers create a style of living that combines beauty and functionality with faith and spirituality. Join author Sharon Hanby-Robie as she shares inspiring narrative, real-life examples, and expert tips on how to live in the true spirit of simplicity.